Catholics

Catholics

A NOVEL

Brian Moore

McClelland and Stewart Limited
Toronto

0-7710-6435-7

Printed and bound in Canada

The Canadian Publishers
McClelland and Stewart Limited
25 Hollinger Road, Toronto 374

Brian Moore is the author of :

The Lonely Passion of Judith Hearne (1956)
The Feast of Lupercal (1957)
The Luck of Ginger Coffey (1960)
An Answer from Limbo (1962)
The Emperor of Ice-Cream (1965)
I am Mary Dunne (1968)
Fergus (1970)
The Revolution Script (1971)

Catholics

𝒯he fog lifted.
The island was there. The visitor walked to the end of the disused pier and saw it across three miles of ocean, riding the sea like an overturned fishing boat. Morning sunlight moved along a keel of mountain, above valleys black as tarred boatsides.

He thought of Rome. Surprisingly, the Order itself had little descriptive information. In the Lungotevere Vaticano he had been handed an out-of-print book: *Weir's Guide to Religious Monuments*.

MUCK ABBEY, Kerry, Ireland. On a small island off the rocky panoramic coastline of the Atlantic ocean known as 'The ring of Kerry.' The Monastery, (Albanesian Order), founded 1216, rebuilt 1400-70, has a dependency, or cell, on the mainland, the priory of Holy Cross, at Mount Coom near the village of Cahirciveen. This priory, sacked by Cromwellian troops, was, in Penal times, a site for clandestine mass, conducted in the open air on a 'mass rock' altar. The Abbey itself (on Muck Island) escaped Cromwellian despoliation and sits on the western slope of the island overlooking a splendour of sea. From the abbey tower the visitor looks down on grey waves which curl on barren rock. The monks fish and gather kelp.

He had telephoned again before breakfast. The pretty girl at the desk in his hotel cranked up an incredibly old-fashioned device to call Exchange. "We're wanting Muck Island. No, Sheilagh, it's all right, it's for that priest who spoke to the island last night."

"There now, Father." He took the receiver. A bell rang and rang.

"Muck Island One," said a crackly voice, out in the Atlantic.

The visitor gave his name. He said he had been asked to call and check on the weather.

"What was your name again, now?"

"Kinsella. *Father* James Kinsella." He had learned his lesson.

"Ah, Father Kinsella. We'll send a boat for you, to be sure. Go down to the pier now, and Padraig will be along shortly."

Gulls, searching the remains of fish, skimmed overhead, dipped to the brackish waters beneath. Behind him, at the end of the road which led to the pier, were three roofless concrete boat sheds, floored with weeds, smelling of urine and sheep droppings. A very old car, which he had thought abandoned, sat in one of the sheds. Yesterday, when he first drove down here searching the fog for a sight of the island, he had looked in at the car. A purple silk stole lay on the front seat. At the hotel, after dinner, he asked who had built this pier. No, the monks had not built it, the Irish Government built it, years ago, before the fishing became polluted. At that time, there were some twenty families living on the island. "They've nearly all come out since. Scattered now, to the four ends of the world."

"Polluted. Does that mean the monks don't fish any more?"

"Ah, no, the fishing is grand again. The water was cleaned up, a while back. The trouble is, it was done too late for the people of Muck. There do be only four families left on the island. And the monks."

The old car he had seen in the boat shed, was it the monastery car?

"It is, indeed. The monks do use it to drive to Cahirciveen of a Sunday. It's twenty miles, Father."

"But, what if the sea is rough, or if there's a fog, and a boat can't come over from the island?"

"Then no Mass is said at Cahirciveen."

No Mass? Yesterday's sights filled his mind; the streets of this Kerry village, grey nineteenth-century facades, market square, grey Gothic chuch, streets built before, and impassable to, today's traffic. Now existing in permanent confusion, cars, buses, trucks, campers, vans, moving in an endless clogged procession in and out of the narrow streets, while on the outskirts more vehicles were bogged in the muddy confusion of improvised car parks and tent villages. And everywhere in Cahirciveen, jammed into the shops and pubs, herded into the main square like beasts on a fair day, the pilgrims. No one knew how many they were on any given weekend, but for months there had not been a room or a bed to rent for fifty miles around. They were Irish, of course, but there seemed an almost equal number from England and Scotland. Others came by car ferry and charter plane from the continent; an emphasis of French, but also many Germans and even some pilgrims from Rome itself. The Americans had flown in two charter groups, many of them old souls who had never crossed the Atlantic before. They came, it seemed, simply to hear at least one Mass, say the rosary, and leave. The uncomfortable local accommodations did not encourage a long stay. It was a phenomenon, even in the history of pilgrimage. There were no miracles, there was no hysteria, there was not even a special fervor. The mood was nostalgic. The pilgrims rose early on Sunday, went in buses and cars to the foot of Mount Coom, five miles from the village. There, they ascended the mountain, on foot, to kneel on muddied grassy slopes, or on shelves of rock, often in the unyielding Irish rain. Most could see the Mass rock and the priest only from a distance, but all heard the Latin, thundering from loudspeakers rigged up by the townsfolk. Latin. The communion bell. Monks as altarboys saying the Latin responses. Incense. The old way.

"No Mass?" he said to the hotelkeeper. "But when they've come all this way, what do they do if there's no Mass?"

"Ah, now, Father, that's a grand thing to see. The pilgrims just stay there, kneeling and saying the rosary. They stay all day, waiting and praying."

"But don't some of them try to go out to the island itself?"

The hotelkeeper laughed, showing gap teeth. "No fear! No boat can land on Muck that doesn't know the trick of it. And the island boats will land nobody without the Abbot's permission. Besides," the hotelkeeper said, serious again. "These pilgrims do be good people. When the Abbot put up a sign in the church here in Cahirciveen saying 'Parishioners Only For Confession,' most of the pilgrims stopped bothering the monks. Mind you, the lines are still long. After Mass, on a Sunday, there do be three monks, hard at it in the church until it's time for them to take the boat back."

"But why do the confessions take so long?"

"We still have private confessions. One person at a time in the box."

Private confessions. *This* was not known in Rome. "What about public confessions?"

"Public confessions, Father?"

"Where the whole congregation stands before Mass and says an act of contrition?"

"Ah, that never took here."

Anger, sudden and cold, made Kinsella say: "It took everywhere else!" Ashamed, he saw the hotelkeeper bob his head, obedient, rebuked but unconvinced.

Yesterday when he first arrived by car from Shannon Kinsella had carried a paramilitary dispatch case, a musette bag, and was wearing grey-green denim fatigues. At the desk of Hern's Hotel, the girl was curt. The hotel was full, there was a two-month waiting list, no reservations had been made for days. "But you took my reservation," he said. "You confirmed it, and the confirmation was telexed from Dublin to Amsterdam Ecumenical Center. This *is* Hern's Hotel, isn't it?"

"What was your name again, sir?"

"James Kinsella. Catholic priest," he said, in the Ecumenical manner.

"Oh, Father Kinsella. Oh, excuse me, Father. We have a room for you, certainly."

Father. In the crowded hotel lobby, every available seat was occupied. Standees circled disconsolately around racks of seaside postcards and shelves of paperback books. *Father.* Sun-reddened faces turned to stare, supercilious of his American accent, his ecumenical clothes. Most of these pilgrims were older than he, old enough to remember the Latin Mass. But there were young ones too, former Catholic Pentecostals, now eager for experience as the *penitentes* of the day. Their scorn towards him, his own scorn in reverse, met him as he went towards the stairs and the privileged bedroom. His friend Visher, a behaviorist, had made a study of current Catholic attitudes towards their clergy. "People are sheep," Visher said. "They haven't changed. They want those old parish priests and those old family doctors. Sheep need authoritarian sheepdogs nipping at their heels from birth to funeral. People don't want truth or social justice, they don't want this ecumenical tolerance. They want certainties. The old parish priest promised that. You can't, Jim."

Waves lapped the slimed boat steps. A new sound entered Kinsella's ear, the pulse of an engine. He looked at the sea but saw no boat. Sound, preceding vision, carrying clear over the whitecapped waves. Pulsing. Coming, coming; the painful confrontation. He and the Abbot of Muck.

"This will not be your first visit to Ireland," Father General said, looking up from the file. It was a statement, not a question, but he felt he should answer it.

"No sir. In my last year at Harvard, I went over there to attend a summer school. The Yeats school, in Sligo. My ancestors were Irish. They came from County Mayo, I believe. It's in the West, where this abbey is."

"William Butler Yeats." The General smiled his faint, Prussian smile. " 'What rough beast, its hour come round at last.' Appropriate. I want you to bury this beast. And I think the way to do that is for me to give you plenipotentiary status. Emissaries who must report back to headquarters, especially young ones, would seem to these old mastodons to be mere novices. I will make clear to this Abbot that you are me. What you decide will be the Order's final edict."

"What about the Father Provincial in Dublin, sir?"

The General sighed. "It seems that he and the Abbot of Muck have a disagreement going back as far as the Pauline papacy. As you know, since Vatican IV, bishops are no longer bound by the orders of provincials. These Irish Abbots are mitred and of episcopal rank. Each is a prelatus nullius, belonging to no one. This one has chosen to ignore the provincial's recommendations. However, he cannot ignore mine." Father General picked up a xerox sheet, a facsimile of an old chapter house record book, microfilmed, its original now destroyed. "The recalcitrant Abbot of Muck," the General said. "Let's see. He is one Tomás O'Malley, now in his sixty-ninth year, the son of a greengrocer. What is a green grocer, I wonder?"

"A seller of vegetables, sir."

"Ah. The Abbot is the product of an Irish seminary, a place called Kilcoole. Prizewinner, Latin, oh, lala! Doctorate in – can't read this script, must be uncial – doesn't matter. Four years at Buckmore Abbey in Kent. Then, Ireland, Dublin, hmm, hmm, and appointed Abbot of Muck. Cast down on some remote little island and abandoned at a relatively early age, it would seem the Order had no great hopes of him. Subsequent life of poverty, thirty monks, fishermen all, income from kelp and dulse, whatever that is, and manure sales – well, that's quite enough of that. You can look this over at your leisure." The General picked up an Order Fact Form. "Now, this gives the age of the abbey, details of grants, etcetera. I think I see why the media people are interested, sick as we all are nowadays for a past we never knew. The monastery was founded in 1216." The General lolled in his Eames chair and looked out of the tall windows of his office. Below was the new pedestrian mall of the Lungotevere Vaticano and, beyond it, the dull, muddy flow of the Tiber. The General's eye moved left to fix on the roofs of the Vatican, and the dome of St. Peter's, immense, even at a distance. "The year twelve hundred and sixteen. Think of it. The fourth Lateran council had just closed. Innocent the Third was in the chair of Peter. And that great monstrosity down the road there, was three hundred years away from being built."

He looked again at the Fact Form. "In the beginning the abbey was not ours. It was founded by some local king, at the behest of Patrick, an Irish bishop saint. The Albanesians petitioned to take over in 1406. Within a couple of hundred years they owned half the lands of Kerry, which is why they have this priory on the mainland. The Abbot of Muck has always had the right to appoint the prior of the cell of Holy Cross at Cahirciveen."

"I believe there is no prior there now, sir."

"That's right, yes." The General consulted the Fact Form. "There are nearby parishes, of course, but the monks still cross to the mainland to say Mass and perform sacerdotal duties. And the changes that have taken place elsewhere in our time have simply been bypassed at Cahirciveen. Our Irish Provincial has made 'suggestions' on four differing occasions, but this Abbot remains blind and dumb. I wonder how long it would have gone on, if it had not been for the tourists? Anyway, it was a B.B.C. crew which did the damage. Latin Mass. Imagine that," the General said, and smiled. "I'd rather like to see one again, wouldn't you?"

"I don't really remember it, sir."

"Backs to the congregation, vestments, *introibo ad altare dei*. And the bell! The Sanctus! Oh, lala, how one forgets. And now it's packing them in. Listen to this. Ferry tours from Liverpool and Fishguard, charter flights from Leeds, Boston, New York – pilgrimage from France – even *bella Italia*." The General's amusement turned to a fit of sneezing. He used a nasal inhaler, then stared again at the brownish waters of the Tiber. "It is cliché to say it was to be expected. Even Vatican IV can't bury two thousand years in a few decades. But, I'd have thought Spain. Or, perhaps, some former Portuguese possession." The General sighed. "We are so infallibly fallible, aren't we? Wasn't it Chesterton who said something about a thing being too big to be seen? Ireland. Of course! Well, here you are. Take the file. Let my secretary have your itinerary. I'd suggest you hop a supersonic tonight and go straight to Amsterdam. It's a formality, of course, but in an affair of this kind everything should be strictly kosher." He smiled. "I'll alert the council that you are my plenipotentiary. After Amsterdam, get straight over to Ireland. Remember, I want this settled by the end of the month."

"Yes, sir."

"Get that old fool down off that mountain, James. And if he gives you any trouble – bite him!"

A fishing boat was instantly in sight, bashing through the tops of the whitecaps, as though in the moment Kinsella had looked away, some Brobdingnagian hand had painted it into the seascape. A diesel-engined ten-tonner, it was built to scramble up and over these grey walls of waves. The wind force increased, sending a great slap of water over the edge of the pier. A black storm cloud filled the edge of the horizon. As the fishing boat approached across the strait, Kinsella picked up his dispatch case which contained the General's letter and an Order Pleni-potentiary, signed in Amsterdam by the four current members of the World Ecumen Council. He walked to the stone steps as the boat cut its engines and drifted out-side the bar. A man in a tweed hat appeared and moved about in the bow. Another stood in the wheelhouse, a stout young fellow in a white turtleneck sweater. Not monks, as he had expected, but islanders, the few fisher families still living on the Abbot's domain. The man in the tweed hat untied a black curragh, which floated light as a mussel shell at the stern of the ten-tonner. Pulling it close, he jumped in, raised long oars and rowed strongly towards the pier, the curragh swinging up like an amusement park gondola to hang on the whitetipped peaks, then fall, dizzyingly, into the trough of waves. The mother boat heeled. With a rattle, an anchor spilled like entrails from its bow, falling deep into the sea. The stout youth came out of the wheelhouse and stood at the side, staring across the water at Kinsella. With his curling red hair, freckled skin, snub nose and white fisherman's sweater he looked like Dylan Thomas.

The curragh, stroked easily now that it had passed into the shelter of the pier, came towards the steps where Kinsella waited. The rower had his back to the steps. Skilful, he shipped the oars as he glided alongside, his hand, with the blind touch of practice, finding the solitary iron bollard at the foot of the steps.

As the tweed-hatted rower turned to look back at the pier, a smile rose on Kinsella's face, an American smile, the currency of greeting. But the rower's eyes moved past him as though he were some idle seabird come to rest on the pier. Eyes swept the pier, the sheds, the road beyond, then, reluctantly, came back to him. "Morning," the boatman said.

"Hello, there." Kinsella, smiling, moved confidently down the last slimed steps towards the curragh. But the boatman shook his head, warning him not to board. The boatman was young, vulpine, with a wild cub's grace. His grey eyes stared, as the eyes of an animal stare from a zoo cage.

"I'm James Kinsella, Catholic priest," Kinsella said, from Ecumenical habit.

The boatman's tongue appeared, round as a teat

between his teeth. Its owner sucked on it, staring, silent.

"*Father* Kinsella," Kinsella corrected himself.

"Ah, come off it," the boatman said, in a soft island brogue.

"I'm sorry?"

"I come for a priest. I can't take nobody else. Sorry, now."

"But I'm the man you came for. I *am* a priest."

The boatman, sucking his tongue again, looked past Kinsella, again searching the pier, the sheds, the road beyond. Then turned to look out at the fishing boat anchored at the bar. On deck, Dylan Thomas raised his head in query.

"Not here yit," the boatman called.

The boy on deck turned and looked back at the distant mass of the island. The fat black cloud was now immense, moving like a dark lens across the sky. The boatman also stared up at the sky.

"Storm coming up?" Kinsella asked.

"'Tis."

"Well, let's go, then. Do you want to see my papers, or something?"

"Come off it," the boatman said, again. He turned away as though Kinsella had already disappeared. Sat in the long, light curragh, gripping the bollard, steadying the craft which bobbed, on the lapping pier waves. Sucked his round tongue for a moment, then yelled across the water. "There's no-o car---aaaa-ar!"

On deck the white-sweatered boy pointed to the sky. "Let's go--o b--aack, Padraig," he called, syllables of sound separated in their transit across the waves.

The boatman abruptly let go of the bollard and took up his oars. Kinsella, irritated, reached down and caught hold of the curragh's stern.

"Let go of that."

"I tell you, I am Father Kinsella. The Abbot is expecting me."

Padraig, the boatman, let go of one oar, seized up a steel rowlock from beneath it and, swift as a biting dog, struck the knuckles which held the curragh's stern. With a gasp of pain, Kinsella drew his hand back. The rowlock snapped into its hole, the oar in it, and, with two swift strokes, the boatman swung the curragh out of reach.

"You don't look like a priest, I just can't imagine you as one." His mother said that, long ago, when in his second year at college he decided to study with Hartmann. Agnostic herself, his mother had continued her son's religious education after her Catholic husband died. She was one for keeping promises. Futures were another matter, as her son found when he told her he intended to become a Catholic priest. Useless to instance that his new hero, Gustav Hartmann, had taken Holy Orders as an Albanesian monk, much as Malraux had become a Minister of State in the Fifth Republic, not for the obvious condition, but as a means towards social action. Which, in Hartmann's case, had made him a twentieth-century Bolívar to this generation of South American revolutionary priests and nuns. The Church, Hartmann taught, despite its history and its dependence on myth and miracle, exists today as the quintessential structure through which social revolution can be brought to certain areas of the globe. But Kinsella's mother, a Liberal, born in the nineteen thirties, did not believe in the combination of Holy Orders and revolutionary theory. She, like that fisherman rowing away from him now, could not see things as they really were.

The curragh tied up beside the fishing boat. The fishing boat's engine came to life, the anchor growled up from the sea. As the fishing boat, turning, churning, headed back towards open waters, Kinsella found himself running, up the pier towards his rented car. Jumped in, went breakneck towards Cahirciveen and a telephone. He was a priest and they had not known he was a priest because the priests they knew wore black suits, or the clothes of old women, long brown habits, sandals, thick belts knotted about with big rosary beads, and he must telephone and order them to turn that boat around and send it back for him at once.

Four miles from the pier, driving through the flat trench landscape of a turf bog, he came, unexpectedy, to a crossroads. A whitewashed cottage stood on one corner, and what seemed to be a larger cottage, also whitewashed, but with a big barn behind it, faced on the opposite corner. On the doorway of the larger cottage was a sign.

P. MCGINN : LICENSED TO SELL WINES & SPIRITS

And a smaller sign, in Gaelic. TELEFON.

Hens rose in fright as he swerved into the cobbled yard. A rooster ran past wattles loose, one skelly eye fixed on the car in wild alarm. Inside the pub it was dark as evening. Two Irish laborers, wearing greasy old black suits, once their Sunday best, now their daily dungarees, white shirts open at the neck, and knee-length rubber Wellington boots. Faces the color of strawberry jam looked up from large glasses of black porter. Behind the small bar, a man, broad as a rainbarrel, wearing a white turtleneck sweater, wiped glasses with a linen cloth. "G'day," said he, to Kinsella. " 'Twill rain, I would say."

"I want to telephone Muck Island."

"You wouldn't get them."

"I'm a priest. They're expecting me."

Strawberry faces of the laborers bobbed uniformly in greeting, as though Kinsella had just entered the pub. "G'day, Father," in unison, they sang. From beneath the bar the proprietor took up a receiver on a hand-crank stand, cranked it up, spoke in a language which Kinsella assumed to be Gaelic. Then: "There, Father. There you are, so."

The crackly island voice. "What? What . . . ? Padraig didn't get you? Ah, sure that's a disaster." And, over the wire, wheezing laughter. "Didn't know you were a priest? Oh, God love us! I'm sorry, Father, but do you see that weather out there, I'm afraid we'll not get you in today . . . . What? What?"

He had to shout. Three faces watched him in that small, hop-stinking room. "Send the boat back! I have to get there today. It's urgent."

"Well, now, Father, the minute the we-----eeee---ather clears, do you heeeee-- do you heeeee--aa-arr?"

Static crackles. Silence. Then a girl's voice. "You were cut off, Father. It's a bad connection at the best of times. I could try them later, if you like?"

"I'll call you," he said, and put the phone down.

Three faces turned to him. Unlike people from more civilised places they did not pretend that they had not overheard. Strawberry cheeks bunched in grins. "So, Padraig refused you," the proprietor said. "Isn't that a good one!"

They laughed. It was.

"Those boys on the island, you see," the proprietor explained. "They never come out, they have no notion that the priests out here do be just like the rest of us, nowadays. Begging your pardon, Father. Are you an American?"

"Yes."

"A grand country, so. You'll get out tomorrow. I'd say 'twill clear."

" 'Twill clear," one of the laborers promised.

"How much do I owe you for the phone?"

"Ah, not at all."

"Well, thank you. Thank you very much."

"G'day. Father."

"G'day. Father."

"Thank you again," Kinsella said.

Outside, in the cobbled yard, hens tacked cautiously around his feet. He looked at the crossroads and there, blurring its outlines, was a rainbow's end. The rainbow arched up and away from this place to disappear behind a brow of mountain. Raindrops spat warnings. Hens stalked to cover. Rain came, wetting to a thick flow. As Kinsella retreated into the shelter of the pub doorway, thunder banged above him. Thunderclouds, massing over the far mountain, advanced to take possession of the sky.

He felt cold. He thought of Hartmann in the rain forests of Brazil. He looked again for the rainbow, but it had vanished, shimmering, in that sudden rain. It had appeared, then disappeared, in this lonely place, a place which now, in its noon darkness, made him think of a Beckett landscape, that place in which Vladimir and Estragon might have waited for Godot. The rainbow had seemed to end, down there, in the center of the white cross formed by two concrete ribbons of road. In such phenomena people once read signs of God's hand. He turned and went back into the pub.

2

*T*he helicopter drifted over the crossroads, the pub, the yard, then, tilting slightly forward, moved downwind to land in a field on the edge of the bog. The rotor blades still turned at take-off speed as Kinsella hurried towards the machine in the afternoon's continuing drizzle, ducking under the great propellers as the pilot slid the door aside and held out a hand to take him up. He sat, buckling his seat belt. The door shut. The green-and-white helicopter, the wind from its rotor blades flattening the whin bushes of the field, rose like some huge dragonfly, its legs, which had bent on hinges under it, stiffening and retracting as it rose in flight. It poised, then, tilting forward, moved up and out. Away.

Below, three faces mooned up, the laborers and the publican. Like children they waved as the helicopter lurched over them. And were gone. Kinsella looked at the pilot, a young man of his own age, dark haired and smiling, staring ahead into the fog and rain. The pilot wore a uniform of black coveralls, but with showy encrustation of gold braid at wrists and shoulders, and, on the peak of his cap, a gold crest. Caparisoned like some admiral of former days, he seemed a personage of importance. Kinsella reflected on the times; cardinals went shabby in mufti, hirelings of all kinds had increased their false panoply of rank.

"Have you even been on the island?" he shouted at the pilot.

"No, but I've flown over it."

Thunder. Lightning sheeted the sky. Within three minutes, they were over the ocean, a rough sea pitted by rainsqualls, but ahead, towards the west, a shaft of sunlight like a stage flood. The pilot pointed to it, grinning and winking to show this was good news. Kinsella nodded. He had waited three hours for the helicopter, fretting, worrying that it would not find the lonely crossroads. In action once more, airborne, travelling at speed, his confidence returned. He would be diplomatic, but firm. With luck, he could have agreement before nightfall.

Now they were over the island, chopping along above a deserted strand, fine grey sand, green grassy dunes, and, at the edge of the sweep of beach, a harbor with a stone pier and two fishing boats tied up at it. One was the ten-tonner which had refused him that morning. Beyond the pier was a ruined medieval castle, built strategically on a green headland, commanding the sea approach. He pointed at it and the pilot, nodding, flew up and hovered the helicopter over the roofless castle maw.

"The fort of Granuaile," the pilot shouted.
"What?"
"Very old. Grace O'Malley built it and lived in it."
"Who?"
"Grace O'Malley. The Sea Queen. Granuaile."

Circling the headland, the helicopter moved down the spine of the island, flying over the village adjoining the fort. The village was a street of a dozen whitewashed cottages, with hen-littered backyards in which were rough stone sheds housing animals and tools. As Kinsella peered down, two small children ran out, stared, then waved. Four of the dozen houses in the street were abandoned, windows broken, holes in the roofs. The helicopter bucked into stormy wind, lurched up and away over tiny fields divided into jagged squares by walls of roughly piled boulders. A road, never paved, led off to two other farms, long abandoned. The helicopter, using the road as marker, curved across the bay, climbed a hillside to a mountain pass, dipped into the pass, was surrounded by walls of grey Gothic rocks, then came out to beauty, on the western slope of the island, to the abbey, as the old guidebook had said, on a headland, *a splendour of sea. From the abbey tower, the visitor looks down on grey waves which curl on barren rock.* The helicopter, strange dragonfly, wheeled and went down on a field to the left of the monastery, rotor blades fanning the grasses, as it came to rest, its strange legs extending, bending to accommodate its weight as it touched ground. The plexiglass door slid open. The rotor blades became visible, whirling, slowing.

"Was it to be the blackberries in the glass jars and the redcurrants in the stone pots? Or was it the other way around, you told me?"

Brother Paul, filled with the demanding urgency which infects the deliberations of small minds, entered the Abbot's parlor, above the chancery of the abbey, without knock or by-your-leave. The Abbot, looking out through the narrow aperture of a thirteenth-century window, did not answer at once. When he did, he said, "Blackberries. Jars."

"Ah, I was right, so I was! I thought it was the blackberries in the glass jars. Would you come down yourself now, and have a look at the fruit?"

"We have a visitor," the Abbot said.

"A visitor?" Brother Paul was alarmed. "Ah, no. Sure, didn't Padraig go out this morning and come back empty? And no other boat could come in, in this weather."

But the Abbot did not seem to hear. "His vorpal blade went snicker-snack," the Abbot said. "It would be a good description of that helicopter out there."

"A what?" Brother Paul bustled to the window. "Oh, that's that yoke from Dingle. I've seen it many's the time passing over here. Is he broke down, or what? Why did he land?"

The Abbot looked at Paul. "Did you not hear it come over, a minute ago?"

Paul blushed. He was deaf, ashamed of it, and a bad liar. "How would I hear it and I down in the calefactory room taking the stems off berries?"

"Go on back down, now," the Abbot said, suddenly weary of Paul. "I had better see to our visitor."

But Paul lingered, his head close to the Abbot's in the vise of the narrow medieval window. "That's not the priest from Rome, surely?"

"I would say it is."

"They'd have to wear special clothes to go up in one of them things," Brother Paul announced. He had not travelled to the mainland in a decade, and had never travelled by air.

"Yes." The Abbot turned from the window. "Go along now and tell Brother Martin to bring the visitor up directly. There is no sense in my climbing the stairs twice."

"I will do that, then," Brother Paul said.

The Abbot turned back to the window. The green-and-white helicopter increased its engine noise, the blades blurring to invisibility. *The frumious bandersnatch*, the

Abbot said to himself. The words fuming and furious made frumious, and frumious it was now as it rose, levitating a few feet above the grass, hesitating as though looking for directions. Getting its bearings, it tilted forward, moving up and out to sea. He will stay the night, the Abbot decided. I will ask Father Manus to get us salmon from the pool. The sky was clearing, but, out there towards Slea Head, the wind force was building. There would be rain.

He heard steps, uncertain, coming up the winding stone staircase beneath his parlor, heard, predictably, Martin's warning. "The ninth step is longer than the others, Father. The trip step, they called it in the old days. Be careful, so."

"Thank you," said the visitor in his American voice, the voice the Abbot had heard on the telephone. Footsteps reached the top of the second flight. Good. It would not do to trip Rome up. "This way, Father," the Abbot called.

To Kinsella, turning and turning in that cold stone turret, to come out through the narrow door into the Abbot's parlor was dizzying, confusing, causing him, at first, to miss his host's welcoming hand.

"How are you, Father." The Abbot's voice was very soft.

"I'm sorry, excuse me, how are you. Good to meet you, Father Abbot."

"So Padraig left you standing on the pier. Oh, he's

thick, that lad. I am sorry you had such a lot of trouble."

"It wasn't his fault. He didn't realise I was a priest."

"But you came on, anyway. Enterprising. Do you know, Father, that's the first flying machine of any description that has ever landed on Muck. You've brought us the symbol of the century. Just when I thought we'd be able to close the hundred years out, and say we missed our time."

"Would you have preferred that, Father Abbot?"

"Preferred what?"

"To have missed this century, to have been born in another time?"

"I should think not," the Abbot said. "If we had lived in the eighteenth century, for instance, our religion was under interdiction by the English. And the nineteenth century was not much better. Unless you had a lust for becoming a martyr, the past was not a time to be a Catholic priest here."

"Yes, of course. I forgot," Kinsella said. "By the way, I have a letter for you from Father General. And this is my Ecumenical Order of Mission. Perhaps you'd care to have a look at them?"

The Abbot would indeed. He stretched out his hand. "An Irish name, you have," he said, as Kinsella undid his dispatch case.

"Yes."

"That is a County Mayo name." The Abbot took the letters, shuffling them like a mailman as he went towards his desk. The Abbot sat, spreading the letters, opening them with a paper knife, reading with attention. As Kinsella tried to read him, noticing first, below the heavy brown woollen robe, black farmer's boots, with double leather soles, great hobnail cleats, and white woollen socks, their tops folded over the tops of these formidable boots. Of course the monks would not wear sandals in this cold. And, similarly, there were fisherman's black oilskins and a fisherman's sou'wester hat, hung up behind the Abbot's door. Those boots; that hat. A practical man. His hands, clumsy on the pages of the Ecumenical Order of Mission, were a workingman's hands, scaled with old cuts, the nails double thick, blue edged. Thin neck, large, glottal Adam's apple, moving in the socket of an oversize collar. The Abbot's grizzled hair was cut very short and, with grey eyes set far back in his skull, separated from his weathered face by a web of white frown lines, he had the look of a sea bird, a fisher hawk, perhaps. Yet, as he put the Ecumenical Order aside and began, attentively, to read the General's letter, Kinsella thought he saw something else. There was, in this humbly dressed old monk, a presence, a power, which recalled to his visitor a painting seen in Venice: Bastiani's portrait of Doge Francesco Foscari, mercantile noble, consummate politician. No, this would not be easy.

"A red-letter day," the Abbot said cheerfully, holding the General's letter up, the better to read it in the window light. "I have been an Albanesian monk for forty-five years, yet this is the first time I've ever held in my hand the signature of our Father General. A red-letter day, indeed. A pity it has to be a letter of censure."

"It is not meant as such, I can assure you."

"I agree. The tone is not unkind," the Abbot said. "But if you have attention paid to you from headquarters and you in a place like this, well, it's a fair guess that you're in hot water."

Kinsella laughed.

"Do you know what we call a place like this, in Ireland? The back of beyond. That's where you are now. The back of beyond."

"It's a great phrase."

"Mind you," the Abbot said. "A few hundred years ago, no place in Christendom was the back of beyond. The Pope, in those days, had a very long arm, indeed. I'll show you something that turned up out in the back there, twenty years ago, in a heap of stuff that was stored away and forgotten. It might amuse you. I mean, the container." The Abbot tugged at the side drawer of his desk. It opened with an unused squeal. Took from the drawer a flat tin on which was a colored picture of a bearded British sailor of former times. And a legend: *Player's Navy Cut Cigarettes*. "In the days when a lot of people smoked cigarettes – fags they called them in Ireland – we had an old lay brother, he was very fond of a smoke and so, when he found this, he thought he was made. 'Fifty fags, Father' said he to me, pleased as Punch with himself. And so," – the Abbot opened the box – "when he opened it up, lo and behold, this was what was in it." The Abbot took out a something, wrapped in tissue paper. He unwrapped it, showing a wax seal. "Have a look at that."

Kinsella took the seal, handling it gently as a sand dollar. Traced in brown wax, the letters:

PIUS
PAPA
II

"In fourteen sixty-three, that seal came here on a letter. We had someone look up the date for us in Rome. In that year Pope Pius the Second wrote to Walter Tobar, the Abbot of Muck, and told him there was a deanship in Kerry reported to be held by a man who had no canonical title. The Pope wanted the Abbot to jump on the man and teach him a lesson. And the Abbot did what he was told."

Laughter, which became a fit of coughing. "So, you see when the word comes this far down the line it usually means trouble for somebody or other. Eh, Father?"

Kinsella smiled and carefully handed back the seal. The Abbot shut it in the tin box. "Cup of tea?"

"Oh, no thanks."

Irishly, the Abbot appraised this, and, Irishly, decided the denial was mere politeness. "Ah, you will!" the Abbot said. He called downstairs. "Brother Martin?"

"Aye."

"Bring us a cup of tea, will you?"

"Two teas," Martin's voice rumbled from below. The Abbot, this settled, again picked up Father General's letter. "I am the sort of person who has to read everything important at least twice over."

"Go ahead."

As the Abbot reread, Kinsella stared about the room. The parlor was large, with a high ceiling, located somewhere over the abbey's sacristy. Three narrow windows gave onto the sea. The furniture, carved by monks, was serviceable, without style. The walls were shelved by books, hundreds of them, spilling onto tables and stacked in odd corners. Surprisingly, there was a special table covered with old green paperback Penguin mystery stories. On the wall, to the Abbot's right, were three stone panels, seventeeth-century Celtic, saints or apostles, figures of beauty, their simplicity emphasised by a horrid oil which took pride of place behind the Abbot's desk, a Victorian painting of a ship sailing in a storm-tossed sea, under heavens rent by the Virgin Mary, prayerful, in blue and white robes, imploring her Heavenly Son for the vessel's safety.

On a window ledge, five large, wooden games boxes, each labelled in Italic script.

CHESS (I)
CHESS (II)
DRAUGHTS (2 Sets)
DOMINOES (I)
DOMINOES (incomplete)

"Do you have television here?"

The Abbot paused in his reading. "Sometimes when there is something big happening in the world, we draw lots and five of us bicycle across the island to Doran's shop on the strand. They have television there."

A pause.

"Not more than five of us, though. Doran's is a small place."

"You know, of course, Father Abbot, that the Mass on Mount Coom and the pilgrims who come to Cahirciveen were widely publicised on a **B.B.C.** television program, a couple of months ago."

"Indeed I do. Didn't we get hundreds of letters about it. I had no notion the Latin Mass was so popular. Do you know, it has given us a new penance. When one of us accuses himself of error before the chapter, he now has to answer some of those letters."

Footsteps. Stout, stertorous, Brother Martin emerged from the stairwell. On a wooden tray were two heavy china bowls, the size of soup bowls. They were filled with strong tea. Milk, sugar, a knife, a pot of blackberry jam. And two plates, each with a thick slice of white bread.

"Did you want an egg with that?" Brother Martin asked, putting the tray down on the Abbot's desk.

"No. We're having salmon with our supper, if Brother Manus can find a few in the pool."

"*Salmon?*"

"Yes, salmon. Father Kinsella has come all the way from Rome. This is an occasion, Martin."

Brother Martin turned to Kinsella. "That bread is our own baking. Irish soda bread." He went back downstairs.

"Poor Martin, he's getting on. We all are, here. I remember, last year, I said to Father Matthew, our master of novices, I said when you retire, we will retire your job with you. For not one recruit did I see coming along. But, do you know, after that television program, we had all sorts of enquiries. I tell you, I could recruit enough young men now to fill a regiment."

"I suppose that's a relief."

"A relief?" The Abbot paused, staring over the rim of his tea bowl. He held the bowl, his index finger cupped over its lip, in the eighteenth-century manner.

"I mean the prospect of being able to get recruits."

"It is not," the Abbot said, putting down his tea bowl and addressing himself to bread and jam.

"You are not anxious for new recruits?"

"I am not. It is a hard life on this island. Fishing, drying kelp, farming a few potatoes. It rains a lot. The monastery is a cold place, there is no way of heating it properly. And we are often hard put to make ends meet."

"But, isn't that the thing about hardship? I mean, men will accept it, if they feel it's for a worthwhile cause."

"Just so." The Abbot spread blackberry jam on his bread. "But the monastic life, as you know yourself, Father, is often something else. I'd break all clergy into two groups. Proselytisers, or prayers. Or, if you like, missionaries or monks."

"Monks can also be missionaries, surely?"

"Not on Muck Island. It takes a special vocation to live in a place like this. Not many have it. I do not have it myself, I sometimes think."

"But you have lived on this island most of your adult life?"

"That does not mean I like it."

"You'd prefer to be somewhere else?"

"I did not say that."

"I'm sorry. Of course not."

"This blackberry jam," the Abbot said, "is last year's.

43

Brother Paul is down in the calefactory room now, bottling this year's jam. He is thinking of his jam. He is not thinking of anything else. I would say Brother Paul has a true vocation for this life."

Kinsella bit into his bread. "And it's delicious jam."

"It is."

"I suppose I am the missionary type," Kinsella said. "My great desire was to be sent to South America."

"Ah, Father Gustav Hartmann. A fine man he must be."

"He is."

"So you went to South America?"

"No. But I studied with Father Hartmann in his class in Boston. He's crippled now, you know."

"No. I did not know."

"He was tortured so many times. The *pau de arara*. Finally, the Brazilian *militares* broke his back."

"I would like to meet him," the Abbot said. "Tell me, does he talk much about God?"

"In what way do you mean, Father Abbot?"

"Ah, I don't know. Forget it. No, what I mean is," the Abbot paused, as though thinking. "Is it souls he's after? Or is it the good of mankind?"

"I would say the second."

The Abbot nodded. "I gathered as much. Of course, I'm not well up on such things. I never had the missionary impulse myself."

"But your zeal for the old Mass, your continuance of the Latin ritual, surely that could be interpreted as missionary spirit?"

"I thought you'd get around to that," the Abbot said, and laughed. "Come on. Let's take a turn outside. The rain has stopped and I want to order up that salmon for our supper. You'll stay the night?"

Kinsella hesitated.

"Ah, you will! What did you tell the man with the helicopter?"

"I said I would telephone him when I'm ready to leave. He can get here in about an hour."

"Time enough, then, to ring him in the morning." The Abbot stood and took his oilskins and sou'wester from the hook behind the door. "Mind the step as you go down."

At the foot of the staircase, a door led to the sacristy. They went through and emerged in the cloister. The Abbot moved briskly, his hobnailed boots loud on the flags of the walk, turning up through a slype and into the refectory, a large bare room around the walls of which were rough refectory tables and benches. In the adjoining kitchen two old monks peeled potatoes from a huge pile. On the hearth hung an iron pot, big as a cartoon cannibal's cookpot. The turf fire gave off a pleasant scent.

One of the old monks looked up and smiled at the visitor. He had two upper teeth, it seemed. "G'day," said he. " 'Twill clear, I would say."

"Ah, yes," said the other old monk.

"Where is Father Manus?"

"I hear tell he's looking for a couple of fish," one old monk said. The other giggled.

"Right, then," the Abbot said. "We'll go and see what he's got."

A door, heavy and stiff on its iron hinges, swung open and they were outside, on a slope of field, looking down at those grey rocks, that splendour of sea. Below, a path led to a small cove. Four black curraghs lay upended on a shelf of rock. A man, in oilskins, carrying a fishing creel, could be seen trudging slowly along the strand. "Come on, down," the Abbot said to his guest. "I think that's our fish."

As they went down the path – "The man with that creel is Father Manus, a very good soul. He is the priest who said the Mass that Sunday when the television fellows came. The other monks make fun of him, now. The reporters tried to interview him on the television but he wouldn't speak." The Abbot kicked a stone clear of the path. "He will speak to you, never fear. He's dying to get a chance at you, I warn you. Still, that's what you're here for, I suppose. Explanations, wasn't that what Father General called them?"

"Yes."

"Maaaaa-nus! Did you get a fish?"

Shouting, his voice lifted and lost in the wind. Implacable, the loud sea on grey-green rocks. The man in oilskins heard, held up his creel.

"We have our fish," the Abbot said.

"Good."

"When Manus catches a salmon he puts it in an ocean pool and the next day, when the boat goes over, we sell on the mainland. Salmon gets a big price. So tonight is a special treat. Eating salmon ourselves. It's things like that – " the Abbot turned on the path and looked back up, his fisher hawk's eyes searching Kinsella's face – "it's the little things that keep us going, here. Like the jam I was talking about. Do you follow me? That is the jam in our lives."

Then turned and went on down, a heavy old man in black oilskins, his head hidden by the sou'wester hat.

While the needs of your particular congregation might seem to be served by retention of the Latin Mass, nevertheless, as Father Kinsella will explain to you, your actions in continuing to employ the older form are, at this time, particularly susceptible to misinterpretation elsewhere as a deliberate contravention of the spirit of aggiornamento. *Such an interpretation can and will be made, not only within the councils of the Church itself, but within the larger councils of the ecumenical movement. This is particularly distressful to us at this time, in view of the* apertura, *possibly the most significant historical event of our century, when interpenetration between Christian and Buddhist faiths is on the verge of reality.*

For all of these reasons, in conclusion, I will only say that, while Father Kinsella is with you to hear explanations, be it understood his decision is mine and, as such, is irrevocable.

English was not, of course, Father General's first language. *Explanations* was an unfortunate choice of word.

Kinsella watched the Abbot jump from rock to shore, landing heavily but surely, striding across the rain-damp sand to meet the other monk whose habit hung down soaking beneath his black oilskin coat. *I would be angered by the tone of that last paragraph. And this is an Abbot who ignored his own Provincial for a dozen years. What if he ignores me? In Brazil, when the Bishop of Manáos denounced Hartmann as a false priest he was banished from the city and, upriver, the villagers refused him food. But he stayed, eating wild roots, waiting in the rain forest until he had sapped the bishop's power. What could I do in this godforsaken spot?*

"Hey!"

The other monk, grinning, held open his creel as the Abbot drew close. Three large salmon, silver-scaled, on a bed of green moss. Grinning, arrested as though in some long-ago school snapshot, the old monk seemed, somehow, to have retained the awkward, boyish grace of his adolescent days.

"Well, Father Abbot, and how will these suit you?" he said, then turned to nod and grin at Kinsella, as though inviting him to share an enormous and obvious joke.

"They will do," the Abbot said, playing his part with great deliberation as he held the creel up. "Yes, I will say they will do nicely, Manus. And this is Father Kinsella, all the way from Rome. Father Manus, our champion fisherman."

"Hello, there," Kinsella said.

"From Rome? So you're the man from Rome. I'd never have thought it."

"What were you expecting?"

"Well, somebody older. A real sergeant-major. And most likely an Italian, or something on that order. You're American, are you?"

"I am."

"Anyway, I'm delighted to see you. Oh, God forgive me, I'm not delighted at all. Sure we're all in fear and trembling of what you're going to do here."

"Manus!" The Abbot, amused, hit Father Manus a thump between the shoulderblades. "Hold your tongue, man. Aren't you the alpha and the omega. When Manus was a little boy they told him it was a sin to tell a lie. I do believe he has not committed that sin since."

"Ah, but seriously, Father Kinsella," Father Manus said. "I have to talk to you. I mean it is an astonishing thing that's happened here. I go over to the mainland every Sunday. And you should just see the way the people react."

"It's beginning to rain," the Abbot warned. "If you want to talk to Father Kinsella, I'd suggest we do it inside. Come along, now."

Setting a brisk pace, he turned and led them back up the path from the beach. The heavy monastery door shut stiffly behind them as they regained the cloister. First to the kitchen, where Father Manus handed over the fish to the old kitchen monks. Then, the Abbot beckoning, Father Manus and Kinsella were led into a small room, furnished with draughtsman's tables and high stools. "All right," the Abbot said. "I'll be referee. Now, Manus, here's your chance. Have at him. What was it you were going to say?"

"What was it I wanted to tell him? What was it I wanted, ah, Lord, I do not know, I tell you, Father Kinsella, since I heard you were coming, I have lain awake at night arguing the toss with myself, saying this and saying that, and – look, it is as plain as the nose on your face, we did nothing to start all this, we went on saying the Mass over there in Cahirciveen the way it was always said, the way we had always said it, the way we had been brought up to say it. The Mass! The Mass in Latin, the priest with his back turned to the congregation because both he and the congregation faced the altar where God was. Offering up the daily sacrifice of the Mass *to God*. Changing bread and wine into the body and blood of Jesus Christ the way Jesus told his disciples to do it at the Last Supper. 'This is my body and this is my blood. Do ye this in commemoration of me.' God sent His Son to redeem us. His Son came down into the world and was crucified for our sins and the Mass is the commemoration of that crucifixion, of that sacrifice of the body and blood of Jesus Christ for our sins. It is priest and people praying to God, assisting in a miracle whereby Jesus Christ again comes down among us, body and blood in the form of the bread and wine there on the altar. And the Mass was said in Latin because Latin was the language of the Church and the Church was one and universal and a Catholic could go into any church in the world, here or in Timbuktu, or in China, and hear the same Mass, the only Mass there was, the Latin Mass. And if the Mass was in

Latin and people did not speak Latin, that was part of the mystery of it, for the Mass was not talking to your neighbor, it was talking to God. Almighty God! And we did it that way for nearly two thousand years and, in all that time, the church was a place to be quiet in, and respectful, it was a hushed place because God was there, God on the altar, in the tabernacle in the form of a wafer of bread and a chalice of wine. It was God's house, where, every day, the daily miracle took place. God coming down among us. A mystery. Just as this new Mass isn't a mystery, it's a mockery, a singsong, it's not talking to God, it's talking to your neighbor, and that's why it's in English, or German or Chinese or whatever language the people in the church happen to speak. It's a symbol, they say, but a symbol of what? It's some entertainment show, that's what it is. And the people see through it. They do! That's why they come to Coom Mountain, that's why they come on planes and boats and the cars thick on the roads and the people camping out in the fields, God help them, and that's why they are there with the rain pouring down on them, and when the Sanctus bell is rung at the moment of Elevation, when the priest kneels and raises up the Host – aye, that little round piece of bread that is now the body of Our Blessed Saviour – holds it up – Almighty God – and the congregation is kneeling at the priest's back, bowed down to adore their God, aye, Father, if you saw those people, their heads bare, the rain pelting off their faces, when they see the Host raised up, that piece of unleavened bread that, through the mystery and the miracle of the Mass, is now the body and blood of Jesus Christ,

Our Saviour, then you would be ashamed, Father, you would be ashamed to sweep all that away and put in its place what you *have* put there – singing and guitars and turning to touch your neighbor, playacting and nonsense, all to make the people come into church the way they used to go to the parish hall for a bingo game!"

Clear: the challenge. His eyes ragebright, a tiny froth of spittle on his cheek as, confused, he came full stop in his tirade. The Abbot stepped between adversaries. "I wish I had all that fire and conviction, Manus. As for you, Father Kinsella, you've just found out we have a lot of sermons in us, here at the back of beyond."

"I'm sorry." Father Manus stared at Kinsella as he would at a man he had, unexpectedly, punched in the mouth. "But, still and all, what I said is only God's truth. Father Abbot will bear me out."

"I don't know what God's truth is," the Abbot said. "Do any of us? If we did, there would be no arguments between us. But it *is* true that a lot of people seem to feel the way Manus does about the old Mass. You know that, of course. That is why you're here."

"Anyway," Father Manus said, his voice loud again. "I think it would be a crime against the people's faith, if we were forced to give up the old way here."

"Manus," the Abbot said, gently. "I wonder would you ask Father Colum to start benediction. I would like to show Father Kinsella around. Would you do that now, like a good man?"

"Yes, Father Abbot, I will do that directly."

"You'll see each other again, at suppertime," the Abbot promised.

Impulsively Father Manus caught hold of Kinsella's arm. "There was nothing personal, Father."

"I know. I appreciate hearing your point of view."

A very dirty monk, face and hands stained with earth, appeared at the door, unaware that he was interrupting. "We found the lamb!" he shouted, then stared slackmouthed at the visitor.

"Good man yourself," the Abbot said. "Where was it?"

"But that's the story of it. In an old byre, by the ruin where the Cullens used to live. And lying down, keeping warm, up against a wee pony."

"With a pony?"

"Right forenenst it. A wee pony of Taig Murtagh's."

"And the pony didn't mind?"

"Divil a bit."

"There's the power of prayer for you," Father Manus said, his good humor restored.

"It took more than prayer," said the dirty monk. "It took the whole day."

"Go along now," the Abbot ordered, and the dirty monk went off with Father Manus. "Are you interested in Romanesque?" the Abbot asked Kinsella.

"Very much."

"Well, I'll show you a couple of things, then. Coming from Rome you will be hard to impress. Oh, what grand sights! I was there at the time of Pope John, years ago, may he rest in peace."

"To study?"

"Ah, no. Just on a holiday. I had been sick and so I was sent off on a jaunt. I went to London, then to Rome and on to Lourdes, in France. My first and last visit to the continent, I expect."

"You enjoyed it."

"Oh, I had a grand time. It was grand to see England again. I served my novitiate there, in Buckmore Abbey in Kent."

"I know."

"Ah, yes, sure you probably know all about me. They make you do your homework well, there on the Lungotevere Vaticano?"

Kinsella, smiling, shook his head. Walking now between cloister arches, Abbot and stranger, the object of constant, covert curiosity. Monks, meditating or reading their office, paced the covered walk, in silence. A light drizzle of rain fell in the rectangular cloister garth. These monks; this place. Most of them would know no other. *Hartmann, in class, sitting in his specially built orthopedic chair, by the window overlooking the Charles River in Boston, his eyes peering down, shaded by thick freckled fingers. There was a two-man skiff on the water below. "The key," Hartmann said, "was when we discovered that no one, or almost no one, in the entire hierarchy of Brazil, Chile, Argentina – no one was truly happy with his posting or his position – once we grasped that truth, we could unlock any door. See that skiff down there? I will bet that one of those two rowers believes that the other man has the better seat. I would bet my life on it. Sometimes to force an issue, you have to bet your life on things like that – things you know nothing about."*

"This way," the Abbot said, leading him into the church. Now, standing in the nave of the abbey, Kinsella felt again that sudden, vivid emotion, that elation in silence of the great bare church at Vézelay, most beautiful of all French Romanesque abbeys, greater even than Autun. Here, as in Vézelay, on this remote Irish island on the edge of the Gothic world, that hush, that bareness which contains all the beauty of belief. Above him, grey stone rose to arch in the Gothic symbol of hands joined in prayer. As in Vézelay, it was an edifice empty as silence, grave as grace. In the chancel, the altar, a bare stone slab on which stood a small tabernacle with a door of beaten Irish gold. Two wooden candlesticks were its only ornaments. No second altar, Kinsella noticed, nothing to conform with the liturgical change of 1966. In the south transept, a small shrine to the Virgin and, above the main altar, a Romanesque crucifix, high on the chancel wall, starveling stone Christ, hung on nails on cross of Irish bog oak.

The Abbot's boots were loud in the nave. "Twelfth century, most of it. But this doorway and these windows are thirteenth century, a transition from Irish Romanesque to Gothic. This cross motif is similar to that in the Monastery of Cong, a Cistercian house. But this one is finer. Probably the finest in Ireland, they tell us."

"It is beautiful."

"A big church this, when you think of the place it's in. Of course there used to be more families living on Muck. The main construction is the original structure. There used to be a holy well on the island, at the time those things were popular. People came over from the mainland by boat to visit it. Little rowboats, made of skin and wood frames, coracles they were called. *Those* people had faith."

"Buckmore is a beautiful abbey too, I hear?"

The Abbot twisted around, head cocked oddly to one side. "It is. Different, of course. This abbey is older and has never been burned. It's one of the few in Ireland that escaped both Henry the Eighth and Cromwell. There are advantages to being remote."

Before leaving Rome, remembering Hartmann's advice in class, Kinsella had mentioned to Father General the question of a transfer. "Sometimes a more rewarding posting brings about a great change of heart," Kinsella said. Father General agreed. "But, only as a last resort. Use it, if absolutely necessary."

"The other thing I wanted to show you, is up there in the south transept," the Abbot said. "Come this way." Genuflecting, moving past benches where four monks knelt in prayer, heads cowled, faces hidden. "All of the Abbots of Muck are buried under this wall. Every one. Can you imagine that? As far as we know, it goes back to the founding. According to the records there are fifty-one laid down there like bottles of wine. And, God willing, I'll be fifty-two. It's rare having Abbots laid down like that. Our abbey in Santiago de Compostela is the only other one I've heard of that has this sort of arrangement."

"If you were appointed Abbot elsewhere, would they not send your body back here to be buried?"

"No. The rule holds only if the Abbot dies here. I'd say my chance is very good. I hope so, anyway. It's an idiotic sort of ambition, but I have it. Funny. This island is not exactly a summer resort, but, do you know, if I go out on the mainland now, I'll not sleep one night over there, if I can get back in. I feel at home here. I am at home nowhere else."

Kinsella stared at his host. Transfer foreseen and forestalled. Did this Abbot leave nothing to chance? And now, as though continuing a guided tour, the Abbot led him away, as monks in twos and threes, cowled, came in at every door until, some twenty-five, they filled the two front benches. From the sacristy, a priest emerged in a cope, silk and gold cloth, richly embroidered by nuns long dead. Before him, a lay brother with censer and chain. *Benediction*. The Abbot, hurrying his guest from this scene of irregularity, pushed open a heavy door in the side of the nave. They went out under raindark skies.

"We have a little guest house, it's not very grand, but there is a hot tub. We'll have our supper at seven. That will give us plenty of time afterwards, if you want to have a chat."

"Thank you."

Following the Abbot along a mud-edged path under

the west wall of the monastery towards a building like a large outhouse alone in a field. "It's off on its own, as you can see." The Abbot turned a key in the door. Inside, a small hall, with an unlit turf fire set in the grate. A coat hanger, a visitor's book on a wooden table, and, on the whitewashed wall, a crucifix made of woven reeds. Off the hall was a bedroom with a narrow monk's bed, a wooden chair, a sheepskin rug on the floor. The bathroom, adjoining, was primitive but adequate; tub, washbasin, toilet, all in a tiny space.

"We will pick you up at six-fifteen. If you are cold, just put a match to that fire."

The door shut. Kinsella moved like a prisoner in the cell-like rooms, then, deciding, stripped off his clothes and ran water in the old-fashioned bathtub. Lay in the tub, the steamy water blurring mirror and windowpane, listening to the cry of gulls, mind idling as his body, gentled by the warm water, grew slack and at ease. The Abbot seemed to be in charge. Father Manus had, no doubt, been brought in early, to dispose of the emotional appeal. There were probably others of his persuasion here. The Abbot used Father Manus to say what he himself is too shrewd to say. Father General's letter is what really interests him, he read it at least three times. He is not angling for preferment or power. Reasonable in what he says; captain of his ship. If this letter from the owners tells him to dump a cargo of ritual, my guess is he will do as he is bid. Hartmann, looking down at the two-man skiff on the

Charles River, saying one must be prepared to gamble everything on a hunch. Will I gamble on the Abbot if he gives me his word? Or is there a grey eminence here, a *Mann im Schatten* I have not yet faced?

Kinsella rose, dripping, from the tub. In the evening air, already cool, the room misted like a steam bath. The towel was rough on his skin. He thought of the confessions; no one had mentioned the confessions. They were, he knew, the greatest danger.

Forty minutes later, when the knock came on the door, he was waiting, dressed in his grey-green fatigues and his flying jacket. Old, grinning schoolboy face, hand clasping his sou'wester, keeping it firm on long grey locks, Father Manus entered the hall, scraping mud clots from the soles of his boots. "Terrible wind! I asked if I could come for you. I am heartsick."

"What?"

"I offered up prayers at Benediction in penance for shouting at you like some wild man from Borneo. As Father Abbot pointed out, sure, I never gave you a chance to open your mouth."

"That's all right."

"It is not all right. It's a disgrace." Father Manus blushed from the neck up, turning to hide his embarrassment, peering out at the gusty rain. "Pelting down. We'll have to run for it. They are all waiting to meet you in the ref."

Slamming the guest house door, Kinsella kept close

to his guide, half running, until they reached the monastery gate. Hurried along the cloister walk to the refectory where the community was assembled, clustered in twos and threes like conference delegates, all whispers and shy smiles as Father Manus led the visitor in. Coats were taken and hung up. The Abbot came forward, genial, linking Kinsella's arm, leading him around, introducing him.

"Father John, Father Colum, Brother Kevin. And Brother Sean. Father Kinsella, from Rome. An Irish name that is? Yes. Is it true what we heard, that Padraig refused to take you on his boat this morning? It is? Oh, glory be! And Father Terence, Father Kinsella from Rome. Terence is in charge of our farm here. Father Alphonsus, Father Kinsella. Did you come all the way from Rome now in that whirligig that landed here today? All the way from Rome, oh, did you hear what Father Alphonsus wants to know! Ah, for goodness sake don't you know that's a helicopter, it could not fly all the way from Rome. Ah, so you came in a bigger aeroplane, did you? I see. From Amsterdam to Shannon and then from Shannon by car. And the helicopter was only because of Padraig. So that was the way of it. Do you know, Father Kinsella, I hear tell there is not a village in Ireland that does not have some class of an airfield near by. Isn't that amazing. Yes, yes.

"And this is Father Matthew, our master of novices. What novices are you talking about, Father Abbot, I think it would be better to introduce me as jack of all trades and master of none. Hardly so, Father Matthew.

Anyway, I want you to meet Father Kinsella, from Rome. Indeed, I know he is from Rome. We all do. You are here because of the doings at Cahirciveen, isn't that so? Yes. It is wonderful the response of the people there on Mount Coom. Wonderful. It would do your heart good to see the piety of the ordinary people. Indeed it would. And I hope – by the way, have you met Father Daniel? – Father Daniel, Father Kinsella, Father Daniel is our business manager. Excuse me, Father Matthew, you were saying? I was saying I hope you are not planning to change our ways, Father Kinsella. In what way, Father Matthew? The Mass, Father. I will be honest and tell you I have been saying a novena for weeks now, hoping that we will be allowed to go on with this holy work."

The Abbot, smooth, led his visitor from danger. "If Father Kinsella would sit here, on my right? And this is Father Walter, my deputy. Sit on Father Kinsella's right, will you, Father Walter, that way we'll have him surrounded by the Muck Island Establishment, haha." Great noise of refectory benches as twenty-six monks sat in to supper. All waited. The Abbot rang a handbell. At once all eyes went to the kitchen door as the two old cook brothers, faces full in triumphal smiles, brought the salmon in. Three fish on three white china platters. Then great bowls of steaming boiled potatoes. Salt and butter dishes. Three big pitchers of buttermilk. When the food was on the table, the Abbot stood. All stood. All prayed:

"Bless us, O Lord, and these Thy gifts, which, of Thy bounty, we are about to receive, through Christ, Our Lord, Amen." Not, Kinsella noted, the approved Ecumenical grace, standard in all other monasteries of the Order. Afterwards, in continuing anachronism, all made the Sign of the Cross. All sat. The Abbot served his guest, then himself. The platters were passed. All ate in silence, quickly, heads bowed to their food. It was the old rule. When the Abbot rose, all rose. "We give Thee thanks, O Lord, for all Thy benefits, Who livest and reignest, world without end. Amen. May the souls of the faithful departed, through the mercy of God, rest in peace. Amen."

Afterwards, the community hovered respectfully, hoping to engage the visitor in further conversation. But the Abbot did not linger. "We will go up now to my parlor for a cup of tea. We are early to bed and early to rise, here. Fishermen and farmers of a sort, as we are, we must use the light God gives us. So, if you will come this way, Father?"

"Goodnight. Goodnight. Off so soon? Goodnight, Father. Sleep well." They watched him go, cheated by this abrupt departure: they had few visitors. Their long-skirted lines parted in polite reluctance as the Abbot, purposeful, led Kinsella back through the cloister, into the sacristy, and up the winding stone staircase to the parlor.

On the Abbot's desk, Brother Martin had left a pot of tea and, incongruously, a plate of lemon puff biscuits. The Abbot took one of the biscuits, holding it up between forefinger and thumb. "Martin is trying to bribe you," he said. "Whenever he wants to soften somebody up, he parts with a few of these. His married sister sends them to him, all the way from Manchester." He munched the biscuit and, munching, moved to pick up the Ecumenical Order of Mission. Frowning, he read it once again. "Sit down, Father. Make yourself comfortable." The Ecumenical Order was tossed on the desk, discarded. Again the General's letter. Read, how many times now? Re-read again, then held up, as though in exhibit. "Is there something I could say that might change your, and our Father General's opinion of these events?"

"Well, I wouldn't know, would I? As you haven't said anything yet."

The Abbot laughed as though this were some extremely subtle joke. "Do you know what they are calling you, over there in the refectory, Father?"

Kinsella waited, smiling at his host.

"The inquisitor." The Abbot laughed. "I thought that was good."

"Hardly an inquisitor."

"Why not? Didn't the Inquisition came around to seek out doctrinal error and punish it?"

"My mission is not punitive."

"Not yet. But what if the heresy continues?"

"Look," Kinsella said, slightly irritated. "This is the end of the twentieth century, not the beginning of the thirteenth. How can we even define what heresy is today?"

"Yesterday's orthodoxy is today's heresy."

"I wouldn't say that, Father Abbot."

"Then what have you got against us saying the Mass in the old way?"

"We are trying to create a uniform posture within the

Church. If everyone decides to worship in his own way – well, it's obvious, it would create a disunity."

"Exactly," the Abbot said. "Breakdown. The loss of control. Look, I agree. There must be discipline. Dish of tea?"

"Thank you, yes."

"Milk and sugar?"

"Black."

The Abbot poured and passed the bowl of tea to his guest. "Explanations," the Abbot said. "Father General seems to feel they would be in order. Very well. I will try to explain why we kept the old Mass here. Will I tell you why?"

"Yes, I would like it – yes, please do."

"Did you know that Ireland used to be the only country in Europe where every Catholic went to Mass of a Sunday? Everyone, even the men?"

"Yes. I was here some years ago. In Sligo."

"Were you, now? Well, anyway, when this new Mass came in, we tried it, we did what we were told. But we noticed that the men would come into Cahirciveen with their families and stand, smoking and talking, outside the church. When Mass was over, they took their women home. Now, I thought that was a bad sign. I mean, this is Ireland, after all. I wrote our Father Provincial about it. He wrote back that the new Mass was popular every-where else. Well, I did not know what to do. We were losing our congregation, hand over fist. I said to myself, maybe the people here are different from the people in other places, maybe they will not stand for this change. After all, what are we doing, playing at being Sunday priests over there on the mainland, if it's not trying to keep the people's faith in Almighty God? I am not a holy man, but, maybe because I am not, I felt I had no right to interfere. I thought it was my duty, not to disturb the faith they have. So, I went back to the old way."

"Then what happened?"

"Nothing happened."

"But it must have been noticed. There must have been talk in the diocese?"

"I suppose there was. But people are not well informed on liturgical matters. I think the people thought because we are an old order we had some special dispensation to do things the old way. Anyway, the old way became very popular, after the word got around."

"And, soon, you had thousands coming to Mass every Sunday."

"That is not so," the Abbot said. "For a number of years we did not have many extra people. Some older people from parishes about. But it was just lately it caught on. It was the tourists. Ireland is choked with tourists now in the summer months. I blame those new planes, those Supers, or whatever you call them."

"So, it was only last summer that you moved out of the priory in Cahirciveen and began saying Mass on Mount Coom?"

"You are well informed. I am not surprised. Our Father Provincial, in Dublin, is not what you would call an admirer of mine."

"On Mount Coom," Kinsella said. "You decided to say Mass on the Mass rock. According to my reading, the Mass rock, in Penal times, was associated with rebellion. Mass was said there, by outlaw priests, in secret, with some member of the congregation on the lookout in case the English soldiers came."

"The Mass rock was a mistake," the Abbot said. "At the time I did not think of the connection. I was just trying to accommodate the crowds."

"You accepted a gift of loudspeakers from the merchants of Cahirciveen."

"It is customary to accept gifts which aim at enhancing worship."

"But, loudspeakers," Kinsella said. "Surely, it has occurred to you that Mount Coom has become a place of pilgrimage?"

"Do you mean a sort of Lourdes?"

"As Lourdes used to be. Lourdes is no longer in operation."

"We are not at all like Lourdes. There are no miracles. We just say Mass."

"And hear private confessions. Which is not known even now, in Rome. I only found it out by accident, myself, the other day in Cahirciveen. As you know, private confessions have been abolished, except in cases of special need where the sin is so grave that private counsel is necessary."

The Abbot frowned. "All mortal sins are mortal to the soul. I find these new rulings difficult to apply."

66

"To begin with, as you know, the category of mortal or venial sin is no longer in use."

"But what am I to do?" The Abbot seemed suddenly distraught. "The people here still think it is a special sin to molest a child, to steal a man's wife, to marry in sin – ah – a whole lot of things! What am I to do if the people still believe that sin is mortal?"

"I know it must be difficult. But the retention of private confessions would be a serious mistake. The idea of Catholics confessing their sins in private to a priest has been distasteful to other groups within the Ecumen brotherhood. Now that the easier form has been sanctioned by Vatican IV – you have read the debates, surely?"

"I have, indeed," the Abbot said. "I know that I am not in step, in the matter of confessions. But, remember, I tried to limit the confessions to people from our parish. It was all part of the same thing. We did not want to disturb the faith of the local people. Still . . . ." The Abbot paused and looked searchingly at his visitor. "You said yourself that Rome did not know about the private confessions. You were not sent here because of that?"

"No."

"Why were you sent, Father Kinsella? What, in particular, caused this – ?" The Abbot picked up Father General's letter.

"American television is planning to do a special one-hour program on what has happened here. Did you know that?"

"So that's it!" The Abbot made a fist of his right hand

and hit the top of his desk. "The damned television! I did not want television here. I will ban them. I was dead against it from the start."

"Even the President of the United States can't ban American television. If the networks want to televise what's going on here, it will be done. And it will be seen all over the world."

"I warned our monks and I told the merchants at Cahirciveen the self-same thing, I said don't have anything to do with those telly people, just tell them it's none of their concern. I refused them permission for any filming on Church property."

"It didn't do much good, did it? Don't you see that even your action in refusing to let these ceremonies be filmed can lend a significance to them that you never intended? A program in the wrong hands, about this subject, could be made to look like the first stirrings of a Catholic counter-revolution."

"Ah, now begging your pardon, Father Kinsella, I find that very far-fetched."

"Far-fetched? To the enemies of the Church, won't it seem that you have acted in direct contradiction to the counsels of Vatican IV?"

The Abbot stared at the fire. In the reflected light of the flames, his features seemed grey as a plaster cast. "I didn't think of myself as contradicting Rome. God forbid."

"I am sure you didn't. And I have been sent here, simply, to clarify things. To explain Father General's concern. And to ask you, for the greater good, to stop this Mass, and these private confessions, at once."

The Abbot, hitching the skirts of his robe, leaned towards the fire, staring at the flames. Kinsella stood. He began to speak, a pulse trembling in his throat, his voice loud in the room, the voice of a believer, telling his true creed. "Father General, in his letter, mentioned the *apertura* with Buddhism, which, of course, you've read about. Perhaps it seems to you that this has nothing to do with life here on this island, but, believe me, it has. Father General is president of the special Ecumenical Council which will inaugurate the Bangkok talks next month. It is the first time an Order head has been so chosen and any scandal about the Albanesians at this time could, as you can guess, be extremely embarrassing to Father General at the talks. He was anxious that you understand he is in a very delicate stage of these negotiations. The *bonze* demonstrations at Kuala Lumpur are, we feel, only a beginning of the opposition tactics."

The Abbot swivelled in his chair, staring up at his visitor. He did not speak. Then, rising, he walked to the windows of his parlor. The faded light of an Irish summer's evening washed a late northern brightness into the room. Through narrow windowpanes, the Abbot stared at the sky. Grey storm clouds sailed west towards America. The sky, abandoned, was bled white by a hidden sun. "I envy you," the Abbot said. "I have been a priest for forty-odd years but I have never been sure why. It must be very rewarding to feel that one's actions might actually change something in this world of ours. If I ask you a question, I hope you won't be offended. But, when a young fellow like you kneels down in church, do you pray? Do you actually say prayers, things like the Hail Mary, the Our Father, and so on?"

"Are you asking me what do I believe?

"Yes, if you wish. There is a book by a Frenchman called Francis Jeanson, have ever you heard of it? *An Unbeliever's Faith,* it is called."

"I have not read it."

"It is interesting. He believes there can be a future for Christianity, provided it gets rid of God. Your friend, Father Hartmann, has mentioned Jeanson in his own writings. The idea is, a Christianity that keeps God can no longer stand up to Marxism. You have not heard of the book?"

"Yes, I have heard of it." Kinsella said. "But I have not read it."

"A pity. I wanted to ask you – the Mass, for instance. What is the Mass to you?"

Kinsella looked at the Abbot, as the Abbot stared out at the evening sky. Now was the time for truth, if only a cautious part of the truth. "I suppose, the Mass to me, as to most Catholics in the world today, is a symbolic act. I do not believe that the bread and wine on the altar is changed into the body and blood of Christ, except in a purely symbolic manner. Therefore, I do not, in the old sense, think of God as actually being present, there in the tabernacle."

The Abbot turned from the window, head cocked on one side, his hawk's features quizzical. "Isn't that remarkable," the Abbot said. "And yet you seem to be what I would call a very *dedicated* young man."

"In what way is it remarkable, Father Abbot? It's the standard belief, in this day and age."

"Or lack of belief," the Abbot said. "I think I was born before my time. A man doesn't have to have such a big dose of faith anymore, does he?"

Kinsella smiled. "Perhaps not." He had been about to add that today's best thinking saw the disappearance of the church building as a place of worship in favor of a more generalised community concept, a group gathered in a meeting to celebrate God-in-others. But decided that, perhaps, the Abbot was not ready for that step.

"Yes," the Abbot said. "I see now why the old Mass is *non grata*. And why you're here to tell us to cease and desist."

"My job is, primarily, to explain the situation – including the special problems facing the Order at present – and, of course, to help handle any transitional problems which might arise with tourists or press."

"You mean when we give up the old Mass?"

"Yes."

"And if I choose to retain it?"

"I hope that won't be the case."

"But you are the General's plenipotentiary," the Abbot said. "If it *is* the case, then you have authority to act against me."

"Yes, I do."

"I don't know why I'm asking," the Abbot said. "The letter made that quite clear. I must be a glutton for punishment."

"On the contrary, you seem to me a very reasonable man. And as an Abbot, with episcopal powers, you realise better than I do the need for seniors in our Order to act in concert and set an example."

"Now, now, hold on, hold your horses," the Abbot said, smiling. "I've had a terrible lot of sermons thrown at me these last weeks. I know what you're going to say, and so on and so forth. But, right now, what I need to do is sit down and think about this letter from Father General. I believe I will do that. We can talk in the morning. Will that be all right?"

"Of course."

"We'll not keep you here for ever, don't worry. Padraig will take you back to the mainland any time you want to go."

"Fine. No hurry."

The Abbot picked up the poker from the grate and hammered on the flagstones. "Martin?"

Below, a voice: "Yes, Father Abbot."

"Will you take our visitor to his quarters?"

Turned to Kinsella, holding out his hand. "Sleep well, Father. And thank you for coming to Muck. I'll be along to take you to breakfast in the morning. Would eight suit you?"

"Fine."

"Martin?"

"Yes, Father Abbot." Brother Martin was now at the head of the stairwell.

"Put a light on the west wall. Father Kinsella is not, like yourself, some class of a night cat."

Brother Martin laughed, as at an old joke. "This way, Father."

Stertorous, a noise like a man blowing on a fire to redden coals, why must they pick this overweight monk for the heart-hurting job of ascending and descending these winding turret stairs? Down, down, behind Brother Martin, gazing at the shiny tonsure on the back of his skull. Through the musty camphor smell of the sacristy, into the cloister walk, Brother Martin, by now wheezing in a frightening manner. At the west entrance an unoiled door opened with a scream of hinges and a monk, wearing a heavy frayed overcoat over his robe, his face half hidden by a full red beard, came out, beckoning. "Father Kinsella?"

"Yes."

"There was a telephone call for you."

"This is Brother Kevin," Brother Martin said.

"'Twas a call from Dingle. The helicopter company. Did you want to ring them?"

"Maybe I'd better."

"Go along then, Martin. I'll take Father Kinsella back." Gripping Kinsella's arm. "Come in, come in."

And shut the screaming door. The room was like a bunker, a narrow window twelve feet long by two feet wide stretched along one wall, giving on a view of mountains, and a cove where curraghs were drawn up on the strand. Papers, manila folders, a short-wave radio and a telephone were jumbled on a long wooden table. The walls were lined with red and white buoys, lobster creels, fishing tackle of various sorts.

"I admit it's a shambles," said the red-bearded monk and now Kinsella recognised the crackly, humorous voice he had spoken to from the pub and from Hern's Hotel. "Will I get you Dingle?"

"Yes. Western Helicopters. Dingle 402, I think."

"That's right. Dan Gavin runs that outfit. I know him." He cranked the handle. "Would you get us Dingle 402, Sheilagh? Thanks, Sheilagh."

He turned to look at Kinsella. "Do the priests in Rome not dress like priests any more?"

"Clerical dress is optional, except on special occasions."

"That's a grand outfit *you're* wearing. Dashing! You look like a soldier boy."

The phone rang. The red-bearded monk handed over the receiver. Kinsella's pilot was on the line. "Yes, I called earlier, Father. We have a report that the island will be socked in around noon. Bad storm off the coast of Spain, coming up fast."

"By noon?"

"Yes. Mightn't even be able to get off by boat after that. Gale-force winds forecast for all of Kerry."

"I see." Held the phone, stared at by the red-bearded monk as, furious, his mind raced through a scenario. "All right," he said. "See if you can come in at nine, okay?"

"Same spot?"

"Right."

"Nine o'clock, then. Will do."

"Goodnight. And thank you."

Redbeard's lips went wide in a grin. "So you're leaving us in the morning, then?"

Kinsella smiled, but did not answer.

"Well, I suppose you'll be wanting to get back to your quarters. I'll show you the road. This way."

The door screamed. They went across the cloister and out at the west gate. Pre-darkness, a failing of light, dimmed the summer sky above them. The wind was strong, blowing the grasses flat along the edges of their muddy path. The red-bearded monk unlocked the guest house door. "Good night, sleep tight and don't let the bugs bite," he said, and cackled childishly.

"Good night. Thank you."

"Don't worry, there are no bugs at all. Not even bed-bugs."

Kinsella locked himself in: he did not know why. Suddenly, he felt tense. The helicopter might be a mistake; it might have been wiser to remain passive, allowing the element of chance, the weather, to lay its onus on the Abbot. Kinsella went into the bathroom and brushed his teeth, then shaved for the second time that day. He stripped and, putting on his one-piece sleeping suit, lay on the narrow bed. With a fanatic like Father Manus, or even that very tall old man, the master of novices, your opposition was in the open, and less dangerous. What *did* the Abbot think? The one argument which seemed to have some effect on him was when he stared at the fire and said, "I didn't think of myself as contradicting Rome. God forbid." Obedience: in the end it was the only card. *Tu es Petrus*. And on this rock I will build my church. And the gates of hell will not prevail against it.

The wind had set up a small rattle in the window-frame. Below on the rocky bluff, constant as a ticking clock, the sound of waves, washing on shore. And then, startling as is any human sound in a wild place, Kinsella heard a voice, singing out a hymn.

> "Faith of our fathers living still
> In spite of dungeon fire and sword.
> Oh, how our hearts beat high with joy
> Whene'er we hear that glorious word.
> Faith of our fathers, holy faith,
> We will be true to thee till death,
> We will be true to thee till death."

When the verse ended, he jumped from his bed and ran to the window. No one. Grassy slopes leading to rock-strewn shore. Yet the voice had been close. And now, it began again.

> "Our fathers chained in prisons dark
> Were still in heart and conscience free."

Ran to the front door, unlocked it and went out. The light on the west wall, requested by the Abbot, shone down, casting its beam all along the path and the shore. Where was the singer?

"How sweet would be our children's fate,
    If they, like them, could die for Thee.
    Faith of our fathers, holy faith,
    We will be true to thee till death.
    We will be true to thee till death."

Silence. He stared about him, wind whipping his light zycron sleeping suit, his hair blowing in thick curls about his face. What about the dungeons into which our fathers' faith put so many poor souls? he wanted to shout. Sing along, you bastard, sing along, it will take more than songs and tricks. I have the power to order, to alter. He went back into the guest house and locked the door. Lay down, reviewing the conversations, the Abbot's remarks, the options. Towards midnight, he set his mind to wake at seven. He turned on his right side. Obedient, his mind admitted sleep.

At midnight, the Abbot left his parlor and went down the winding stairs. He was aware that rules were being broken; certain monks were not in bed. He knew this, without evidence, but as surely as he knew most other details of life on Muck. In time of crisis such things were to be expected. But not permitted. As he went through the sacristy, putting out the lights behind him, he heard a noise in the church. He went in through the door at the south transept.

There were no lights in the church, save a candle before the small shrine to the Virgin, and the red sanctuary lamp over the main altar. In the chancel Father Walter and Father Manus knelt side by side, in semi-darkness, their arms outstretched in that painful posture of adoration which simulates the outstretched arms of the crucified Christ. Behind them, less spectacularly at prayer, were Brothers Sean, John and Michael, and, sitting on a bench, two of the oldest monks, Father Benedict and Brother Paul. The Abbot's entrance was not noticed, although he made no effort to walk softly. A sign, he knew, that others were expected.

"Father Walter," the Abbot said, in a loud voice.

All eyes sideshot to south transept. All saw the Abbot who saw all. Father Walter, lowering his praying arms, rose stiffly from his knees and marched to the rear of the church to confront his superior. Father Manus was at once joined in cruciform adoration by old Father Benedict.

The Abbot put his arm on Father Walter and drew him out into the night damp of the cloister walk.
    "So you are in on this?"
    "Have you good news for us, I hope, Tomás?"
    "I have no news. I asked you a question."
    "Yes. I am the ringleader."
    "You are not. Adding a lie to your sins will not help whatever foolish aim you have in mind."
    "You know very well what I have in mind. It is what we all have in mind."

"Is it. Do you know *my* mind?"

"Asking God's help is not a sin."

"Breaking the rule of obedience is."

"Tomás, you are not going to be vexed with us, are you?"

"I am very disappointed. I want you to go in there and tell those others to get off to their beds at once."

Father Walter's face went happily into a smile. "Our prayers are answered, so!"

"They are nothing of the sort. There is work to be done in the fields and in the abbey. The boats will have to be out to the pots and back by noon. The mackerel are running off Slea Head and I want nets out. We live by work, as I have said a hundred times. We are not a contemplative order."

"This is a case when only the power of prayer can help."

"You can not run a monastic community like a holiday camp, Walter. People taking it into their heads to stay up all night without a by-your-leave or a with-your-leave. I asked everybody to behave as usual, while this visitor was in the house. I am disappointed in you, Walter."

"It was my fault, so it was, Father Abbot."

"I know who the ringleader is, there is not any sense in you pretending you are he. What you are is my deputy. If I cannot trust you to carry out an order, then where am I?"

"I am sorry, Tomás. I will get them off to bed."

"I do not want to see them ten minutes from now. And I want no holy vigils in cells, do you hear? The holiest thing every man jack of you can do is turn out fit to work in the morning. Goodnight, now."

"Goodnight and God bless you," Father Walter said.

The Abbot crossed the cloister to a bay where there was an ambry used for storing wood. He checked the lock which Brother Kevin had reported as broken. It was broken. He heard them in the cloister walk behind him, but did not turn around until all was silence. Then he went back into the church.

A dark church: the flickering oil flame of the sanctuary light over the altar, the gutter of one fat five-day candle beneath the small shrine to Our Lady. The Abbot genuflected, from habit, as he faced the chancel, then sat down heavily on one of the benches near Our Lady's shrine. Looked at the candle, beneath the shrine. Father Donald lit that. Every year, Father Donald's old mother sent him a little money to buy things like warm gloves and mufflers. Every year, he spent it in candles lit, before Our Lady's shrine, in time of trouble. Candles as at Lourdes. "Lourdes is no longer in operation," the Abbot's visitor had said tonight. Lourdes, that sad and dreadful place; the Abbot thought of his own visit to Lourdes, remembering the thousands on thousands of banked candles in the grotto where the Virgin was supposed to have appeared to an illiterate French girl. With four other priests he had arrived on a pilgrimage excursion and, on the first morning, visited the shrine to see the myriad crutches and trusses hung on the grotto wall, the medical bureau with its certifications of 'miraculous' cures, the tawdry religious supermarkets, crammed with rosaries and statuettes, the long lines of stretchers and wheelchairs on which lay the desperate and the ill, the stinking waters of the 'miraculous' bathing pool. At noon, the Abbot fled to his hotel room, where, pleading dysentery, he shut himself up, seeing no one, until it was time for the excursion train to leave. Two days in that room, trying not to think of what he had seen, trying to say his prayers.

It was not the first time. There had been moments before, sometimes hours, even days, where, back on Muck or in some church on the mainland, that bad time had come on him, that time when, staring at the altar, he knew the hell of the metaphysicians: the hell of those deprived of God. When it came on him, he could not pray, prayers seemed false or without any meaning at all. Then his trembling began, that fear and trembling which was a sort of purgatory presaging the true hell to come, the hell of no feeling, that null, that void. A man wearing the habit of a religious, sitting in a building, staring at a table called an altar on which there is a box called a tabernacle and inside the tabernacle there is a chalice with a lid called a ciborium, and inside the ciborium are twelve round wafers of unleavened bread made by the Sisters of Knock Convent, Knock, Co. Mayo. That is all that is there. That is all that is in the tabernacle in this building which is said to be the house of God. And the man who sits facing the tabernacle is a man with the apt title of *prelatus nullius,* nobody's prelate, belonging to nobody.

Not God's Abbot, although sometimes he tries to say the words; "Our Father Who Art in Heaven," but there is no Father in heaven, His name is not hallowed by these words, His kingdom will not come to he who sits and stares at the tabernacle; who, when he tries to pray, enters null; who, when in it, must remain, from day to day, weeks becoming months, and, sometimes, as after Lourdes, a year.

Lourdes was the worst time: it was not the first and it would not be the last. If he prayed. So the Abbot avoided prayer. One could pretend to a preference for private devotions. One's Mass could be said alone. He no longer read his daily office. As for public prayers, in a community like this there were always others, greedy to lead. Sometimes, one had to say a grace. One said the words, but did not pray. If one did not risk invoking God, one did not risk one's peace of mind. He was needed here. He did his work. He did his best. But did not pray. He had not prayed now for, well, he did not want to think. A long time, yes. Some years.

Tonight, he sat in the church, as a man sits in an empty waiting room. After some minutes, footsteps sounded in the nave. The Abbot did not turn around. He, whom he expected, had come.

Father Matthew, six feet five inches tall, the biggest man on Muck, marched up the center aisle of the church with a tread like an armored knight. Master of Novices with no novices to master, an authoritarian figure denied the command he might have graced, in Kilcoole, long ago, he and the Abbot had been seminary classmates, and rivals for the Latin prize. At that time, the world was at war, and Winston Churchill had to deal with a stubborn, righteous, very tall, young French general, who led the Free French Forces under the banner of the Cross of Lorraine. Then, as now, physically and in temperament, Father Matthew resembled General de Gaulle. And then, as now, the Abbot knew what Churchill meant when he said "the cross I have to bear is the Cross of Lorraine." Unyielding in his scruples, militant in his devotions, Fathew Matthew, even in his age, was no man to cross. Now, his hoar-white hair and beard making him a ghost in the near-darkness, he marched towards the altar, his lips moving in muttered devotions.

"Father Matthew!"

Father Matthew stopped, as though brought up short by an invisible fence. His great head probed the shadows. "Ah, Father Abbot. And where are the others?"

"What others?"

"The vigil."

"*What* vigil?"

"It is a vigil of devotion in honor of Our Lady, offered up for the purpose of preserving the Latin Mass on Mount Coom and here on Muck."

"The other monks are in bed. I sent them to bed."

"And why did you do that, Father Abbot?"

"Because I am in charge here."

Father Matthew sighed, audibly.

"Father Matthew, it is some years now since I have taken it upon myself to rebuke you. The last thing in the world I want is to reopen our disagreements of former days. There is work to be done tomorrow. You will please go to your bed."

"I have made a solemn promise to Our Lady to hold a vigil in her honor this night."

"When you were ordained as an Albanesian monk, you made a solemn promise to God to obey your superiors. Go to bed."

Father Matthew stood immobile, tall as a round stone tower. "May I ask, then, Father Abbot, what is your decision about Mount Coom?"

From his bench, the Abbot looked up coldly at the figure in the aisle. "I am informed by Rome that the Mass is now merely symbolic. Do you understand what I am saying?"

"That is heresy, pure and simple!"

"Why is it heresy, Father Matthew?"

"Because the Mass is the daily miracle of the Catholic Faith. The Mass, in which bread and wine are changed by the priest into the body and blood of Jesus Christ. Without that, what is the Church?"

"Then our belief in Jesus Christ and His Church depends on a belief in miracles. Is that it, Matthew?"

"Of course that is it! St. Augustine said, 'I should not be a Christian but for the miracles.' And Pascal said, 'Had it not been for the miracles, there would have been no sin in not believing in Jesus Christ.' Without a miracle,

Christ did not rise from His tomb and ascend into heaven. And without that, there would be no Christian Church!"

"Our visitor brings an order from our Father General. Would you obey that order, Father Matthew, even if that order instructed you to consider the Mass not as a miracle, but, let's say, just a pious ritual?"

"Far be it from me to speak out against my superiors," Father Matthew thundered, "but I am ashamed to hear that talk coming from you – and under God's roof."

"Are you, now?" the Abbot said, suddenly weary. "But, on the other hand, it seems you are not ashamed to *act* against the orders of your superiors. Even to the point of disobedience."

"I do not consider that I have ever been disobedient to our rule."

"You were told there were to be no vigils or special observances tonight."

"I acted according to my conscience, Father Abbot."

"Did you, indeed? And was it your conscience that sent you down to the shore, a while ago, singing hymns to annoy our visitor?"

"I sang a hymn, yes. Is he the sort of heathen who would be offended by the singing of a Catholic hymn?"

"Hold your tongue!" the Abbot shouted. "Go to your cell. Tomorrow, at suppertime, I want you in front of the chapter with an apology for your behavior. I have had enough of you, Matthew, all these years. Insolence and insubordination is the opposite of every vow you took when you became a monk. Are you not ashamed!"

"Father Abbot, I humbly apologise to you, since you ask me to apologise," Father Matthew said. The Abbot, in twenty years, had never spoken to him in this tone of voice. Shaken, but anxious not to show it, Father Matthew turned and genuflected to the altar. Rising, he made the Sign of the Cross. "Since you order me to retire, I obey your order." Turning, he walked with heavy steps back down the aisle whence he came. The door at the foot of the nave banged shut.

The Abbot sighed. Years ago, he would have knelt and offered up an act of contrition for his unruly temper. But, years ago, he had felt a certainty about so many things. *Aggiornamento,* was that when uncertainty had begun? Changes of Doctrine. Setting oneself up as ultimate authority. Insubordination. He looked at the tabernacle. Insubordination. The beginning of breakdown. And, long ago, that righteous prig at Wittenberg nailing his defiance to the church door.

The Abbot rose. He did not genuflect. He went down the side aisle and out into the night.

3

*K*insella woke at seven. In the rectangle of window above his bed, the sky was already light. Gulls rode that sky, kites held by invisible string. When, dressed and shaven, he opened the guest house door and stepped outside, he met the rush of breakers on shore, a long retreating roar of water. Obbligato of gull cries overhead, their harsh, despairing scream seeming to mourn a death. Winds whipped like penny tops, spinning the long grasses this way and that. The sky, immense, hurried, shifted its scenery of ragged clouds. From the cove below, four curraghs were putting out to sea. A fifth rode, far out, waiting for the others, as, bending to their oars, monks seal-wet in black oilskins pushed the curraghs stiffly over fence-like waves, moving towards the deeps. The day's work had begun. Kinsella turned back towards the land. He felt the loneliness of islands, the sense of being shut in, here on a barren out-cropping on the edge of Europe, surrounded by this desolation of ocean. Above him now, on a sloping field, four monks, skirts hitched up, spaded heavy shovels full of black earth. From the monastery itself he smelled the delicate scent of turf fires. An old monk, waiting just inside the cloister entrance, saw Kinsella standing outside the guest house, waved to him and began to hurry towards him along the muddy path beneath the west wall of the monastery. The monk was not the Abbot of Muck.

Came closer: Father Manus, tall, white-haired and boyish, with the wanting-to-please smile of the Irish countryside. "Ah, good morning to you, Father. You slept well, I hope?"

"Yes, thank you."

"Father Abbot asked me to find out if you would like to say Mass this morning? It would be easily arranged, so."

Kinsella said he thought not.

"Then we'll put some breakfast into you, will we?"

"The Abbot was supposed to meet me here at eight. Perhaps I should wait?"

"Ah, well, he might be a bit delayed. He told me to look after you. He's trying to get through on the telephone to Galway. We shipped some dulse down there last week and it's still stuck in the railway sheds."

"Dulse?"

"Dried seaweed. It is good eating. They sell it abroad, too. Have you never heard of it?"

"I'm afraid not."

In the refectory, the breakfast plates had already been cleared away. The old kitchen monk put his head around the door. "Two boiled eggs or one?"

"One, thank you."

The second old monk now appeared with a pot of tea and slices of homemade bread.

"Butter, for our visitor. And jam, too," Father Manus said, anxiously.

"I am getting it, so." The old monk sounded cross.

"You see," Father Manus told Kinsella. "We don't eat jam except on special occasions."

"Feast days!" the old monk said, and chortled unexpectedly.

"I will leave you, so, to your breakfast," Father Manus said, withdrawing.

The second old monk approached, bearing a boiled egg on a plate. Kinsella, sensing it was expected, bowed his head and silently said an Ecumen grace. No one said private grace nowadays. Grace was public and used only in mixed Ecumenical groups. The old monk withdrew. The kitchen door shut. Kinsella was alone in the refectory.

It was ten past eight. The Abbot's absence might well be deliberate. *Hartmann, suspended in his back brace, not seeming to be seated, but rather hung in his ortho-*

pedic chair, his freckled fingers knitting and unknitting on the outer steerer wheels. "Almost always, the techniques were the same. When the bishops had decided to deny our requests, we were made to wait. Conferences were cancelled, interviews delayed. Excuses offered without conviction. You must show them that while you are the Revolution and they are Tradition, the Revolution is the established faith and will prevail. Power is the concept they have always understood. Use it, and use it from the beginning." If this monastery was organised as others were, the Abbot would know the exact moment the helicopter was due, might even wait almost to the moment of departure to offer some delaying tactic, or bring a compromise offer into play. It would not do. Immediate compliance could be ordered under threat of transfer. An acting Abbot could be installed at once. There was, however, a complication. The Abbot might not know it, but, under Ecumen Rules, he had the right of appeal to the Amsterdam World Council. He would lose, of course, but the case might drag on for months. And, meantime, he could not be deposed. Such a confrontation was to be avoided. For one thing, it would almost certainly inspire a media circus with the Abbot as martyr. If the Abbot knew these rights of his, Kinsella also knew the catch to them. By Ecumen rules, the Abbot must, before bringing his case to the Amsterdam World Council, first have had a direct confrontation with his Order Superior. That Superior, Father General Humbertus Von Kleist, of the Albanesian Order, Grand Chancellor of the Pontifical Atheneum of St. Vicente, would face the Abbot on his arrival in Rome. The Abbot would need to be strong. Very strong.

But Kinsella felt it would not come to that. There were ways of shading the options, ways of exploring one's adversary's intentions without actually making a committing move.

"Was that egg fresh?"

The Abbot had come into the refectory, without any sound. He stood behind his visitor, thumbs hooked in the broad leather belt in which his rosary was knotted, his face mild in a morning smile.

"Delicious."

"They are our hens. They were not laying last month, but they are usually quite co-operative. I hope you slept well?"

"Yes. And you?"

"I was late to bed," the Abbot said, swinging his leg over the refectory bench and sitting down opposite Kinsella. At once, as though he had been peering through a crack in the door, the old kitchen brother appeared. He set a bowl before the Abbot and poured black tea into it, then went further down the table, wiping the top off with a dishcloth. The Abbot looked at the bowl. "Sometimes I wish my insides were lined with tin, like one of those old tea chests. I have a terrible taste for tea." He looked down the long table. "Brother Pius, get back to your work, if you please!"

"I *am* working," the old brother said, crossly, but

stopped wiping off the table, and went back into the kitchen.

"There is great curiosity," the Abbot said. "The walls not only have ears, they have tongues as well. They announced to me at first light this morning that a helicopter is due in here at nine. Is that right?"

"There is supposed to be a bad storm coming up at noon."

"There is a storm," the Abbot said. "I heard it on the wireless. It will be here some time today. That is sure. There will be rain, starting any time now. But that is nothing new. Rain is what we get most of here, you know."

Kinsella nodded, hoping to encourage further talk.

"So you are off," the Abbot said.

"I hope so."

"Yes," the Abbot said. 'You are right to go. No sense hanging around. You delivered your letter and that's all that's necessary."

"Not quite all," Kinsella said, very carefully. There was a great silence in the dining hall.

"Brother Pius and Brother Malachy, who is in there with you?" the Abbot shouted, suddenly.

"Nobody at all, Father Abbot."

"Well, get on with your work, then. Let me hear some noise."

There was a sudden rattle of pots and the noise of running water. The Abbot listened to be sure it continued. Then, putting his head to one side in his quizzical fashion, he stared at Kinsella. "Not quite all, you said? Was there something else?"

"You haven't told me what you're going to do. I don't feel I should leave until I know that."

"Do?" the Abbot said. "I will do as I am bid. Father General's letter is perfectly clear. No more Latin Mass here or on Mount Coom. No more private confessions. That is his wish, is it not?"

Kinsella stared; the helicopter on its way now, the Abbot's late arrival, this sudden *volte face,* this suspicious obedience. What was the trap, he asked himself, even as he nodded, yes, yes, indeed, this was what Father General wanted.

"Then it will be done," the Abbot said. "I had no right to take upon myself decisions which belong to my superiors. I have written a letter of apology to Father General, which I would ask you to deliver for me."

"Yes, of course." What was the catch? There must be a catch.

The Abbot took an envelope from the inner pocket of his robe. "I have not sealed it. You may read it, if you wish."

Carefully, Kinsella put the letter, unread, in the inside pocket of his fatigues jacket. "Why?" he said.

"Why, what? Why read the letter?"

"No. Why have you acted as you did?"

"Because it is my duty to obey."

"Yes, but, earlier, you felt that it was your duty to disobey – to retain the old Mass and so on."

The Abbot turned and stared at the kitchen door.

"They are very nosey," he said. "Let us go outside. You'll want to be getting your bag, won't you?"

"Yes, of course."

Through the cloister they went, and over to the west entrance. Spits of rain in the wind, as the Abbot and his visitor turned onto the muddy path leading to the guest house. The Abbot took Kinsella's arm. "I did not want to discuss it in front of them," he said, distractedly. "You see, that will be the important part, how I break it to them. Some of them are very devout. They will take it hard. No, it will not be easy at all. To tell you the truth I am a bit nervous about it."

"Perhaps you would like me to break it to them."

"Oh, no, no, no," the Abbot said. "I want you to go. I want you away before they know. Oh, believe me, they would bother the life out of you, if they knew what you and I know now."

Bent his head, and gripped his visitor's arm tightly as they faced into the wind. "You asked why I acted as I did. I do not want you to think it was from an excess of zeal. On the contrary, it was, rather, from a lack of it. However, that's neither here nor there, is it? That is of no interest to anyone but me."

"It interests me," Kinsella said.

"I am not a holy man," the Abbot said. "Far from it. I would not like to fly under false colors. There are some holy men here, I suppose. On Muck, I mean. But I am not one of them. I have become a very secular man. Do you know what I mean?"

"I don't think I do."

"I am a sort of foreman here, a sort of manager. It is not a lot different from a secular job. The monks work hard and my job is to keep them together and see that they make a go of it. It's a simple life, here. Little jokes, little triumphs, little disasters. We're like a bunch of children, we pass the days as if we had an endless supply of them. It's only when someone like yourself comes along that we ask ourselves what are we here for. What good do we do?"

The Abbot stopped outside the guest house door. He turned the key and pushed the door open. "Ah, you are a tidy man. Bag all packed. You travel light. It is the best way. I'll take your bag."

"No, please."

"Very well, so. Let us go along now to the field. It is nearly nine. I want to get you off, you see, and then I have to face up to it. Face the music. It is all in how you tell them. The thing about being in charge is, you must be firm. As Father General is firm. And yourself. What would you have done if I had said I wouldn't follow orders?"

Kinsella laughed but did not speak.

"You are right, better not ask. By the way, what do you want me to say to the press and the telly people if they call up here?"

"Refer all inquiries to me. James Kinsella, Ecumenical Center Information Office, Amsterdam."

"I will do that," the Abbot said. "Let us cut across the field. Do you see them up there, waiting?"

Ahead, in the field where Kinsella landed yesterday, some ten or fifteen monks were gathered, looking about them, oblivious to the rain, scanning the skies in every direction. "They should be at their work," the Abbot said. "Of course they will all be after me, the minute you go. By the way, if they ask you something, do not answer. Let me deal with them."

As they came up the field, the monks turned to look at them. At that moment, above, the sound of an engine. "Your machine is on the way," the Abbot said, looking up.

"I don't see it."

"I do. It is over there. Here he comes. Right on the dot."

Three monks detached themselves from the larger group. The oldest of them, very tall, with white hair and beard, stood straight in the Abbot's path. "Do you have any news for us, Father Abbot?"

"Are the horses brought up from that lower field to take the load of fertiliser over to Doran's?"

"Yes, they are. May I ask our visitor a question?"

"You may not!" the Abbot said. "Let us pass."

Reluctant, the tall monk drew aside. The Abbot, still gripping his visitor's arm, hurried him on. "A holy man that," he said. "But a tiresome one."

"You really *are* expecting trouble."

"Not trouble, no. It is just difficult. Ah! There he comes. The frumious bandersnatch."

Engine noise made all speech impossible until the helicopter had landed and throttled back its motor. "You have my letter, have you?"

"Yes, I have."

"Well, safe home to Rome. And good luck to you, Father Kinsella."

"Good luck to you, sir."

The rain was heavy now as the pilot slid open the plexiglass door. Kinsella shook hands with his host, then, bending low, ran to the machine. The pilot reached out to pull him up. The door shut. The monks, in a ragged circle, seemed to press close. But, at that point the helicopter rose, lurched forward and went out to sea.

Kinsella looked down. The Abbot, standing alone, waved, waved. The other monks bunched in a cluster, stared up at the helicopter as it passed over the abbey tower, out to that splendour of sea. Kinsella saw the old man, a tiny figure on the promontory of land, turn and walk back towards the monastery gate. The monks, moving as in a pack, followed him in.

Heard their shuffling feet, their voices, the whisperings as in church in the moment of talk at the end of the silence of a retreat, the mutterings increasing until, although he knew they were not more than twenty monks, they sounded as he imagined a mob might sound: knowing those who were and were not here, knowing that eight fishermen who always had the least to say in community disputes were out now in their curraghs, serving the sea, a master hard as eternity, but the land was a hard master too, yet all the monks from the farm were here, Terence's crew and Daniel's, who worked packing dulse and gathering kelp, yes, there were not more than nine men missing in the whole community, it would be what happened now that would decide it. What I say now. What I say to them now.

"Father Abbot?"

He turned in the cloister, saw all of them crowding in behind the triumvirate; Matthew, Manus, Walter. It was Walter who had called him.

"Yes, Father Walter?"

"Can you tell us, now? The man is gone."

4

*W*aited till they were all in, lined up in a long queue in the cloister walk. "Yes, I can tell you now. Father General, in Rome, has written me a letter of instruction. It will be obeyed. From now on, the new Mass will be said in English, here and at Cahirciveen. The altars will conform with liturgical changes and will face the congregation. There will be no further private confessions, except in the very special circumstances prescribed, where the nature of the confession warrants private consultation. That is all. We

have our orders and it is up to all of us to carry them out
to the very best of our ability. I am sure we will do that,
won't we?"

He did not look at Matthew, or at Manus, but kept
his eyes moving between Father Donald, who had a
breakdown last year and was subject to sudden tears, and
Brother Kevin, whose hysteria was tight, reined in uncertain check. Something of that nature was what he feared,
but the thing to do now was be firm, disperse them,
reassert the rule of obedience. "And the first thing we
will do," he said, attempting a smile, "is every man jack
get back to work. That is all. Now, off you go."

"That is not all!" Father Matthew, angry as Isaiah,
pointing an accusatory finger, rearing up in his great
height. "Why have you not told the community, Father
Abbot, what you told to me last night?"

"Last night I told you to go to bed. Now, I tell you to
go to work."

The laughter he had wanted, flickered, then stilled.

"You also told me that we are to consider the Mass,
from now on, not as a miracle, but as a 'pious ritual,' I
believe you said."

"That is correct."

"How can a thing be a miracle one day and not a
miracle the next day?"

"Maybe you are a greater theologian than the Pope
or the Vatican Council, Father Matthew. I am not. I am
a monk and I do as I am bid."

"No, no, no, no!" As the Abbot had feared, Father Donald had come to tears. "That is sacrilege, that is blasphemy. No, no, no, I can't be hearing that, no, no!"

The Abbot put his arm comfortingly on Father Donald's shoulders. "Now, Donald," the Abbot said. "You are not yourself, you mustn't be getting excited like this. Come along, everybody. Let's get to work."

"And *I* will not not be put off like that," Father Matthew shouted. "I will not be ordered to believe something which I do not believe."

"No one can order belief," the Abbot said. "It is a gift from God." But even as he said this, said the only truth left to him, he saw in these faces that he was failing, that he was losing them, that he must do something he had never done, give something he had never given in these, his years as their Abbot. What had kept him in fear since Lourdes, must now be faced. What he feared most to do must be done. And if, in doing it, I enter null and never return, amen. My time has come.

Matthew, bent on trouble, began again. "You can all see what is being proposed here. It is a denial of everything the Mass stands for."

The Abbot held up his hands, commanding silence. There was silence. He turned and held open the door which led into the nave. "Please. Let us go into the church."

Stood, holding the door for them, as they moved past him, his eyes on their faces, these faces he knew better than his own, seeing every shade of wavering, from confusion, to doubt, to anger at him, to fear, to Father Donald's dangerous tears and Brother Kevin's hysterics, tight on snaffle, a horse ready to bolt. He entered behind them and shut the door. Moved past them in the aisle, going up into the great vault of the nave, moving in that silence, in the grey light of this place where he had spent the longest years of his life, this place where his body would lie, this place he feared most. He entered the chancel. He faced the altar.

"A miracle," he told them, "is when God is there in the tabernacle."

"But you said the opposite, you said that the sacrifice of the Mass is just ritual, that bread and wine remain bread and wine, that there are no miracles!"

Matthew, thundering: righteous, wronged. The Abbot, his back to all of them, heard their stiff intake of breath, the fear of their lives at these words, said in this place. He stared at the golden door of the tabernacle. His fear came. "Prayer is the only miracle," he said. "We pray. If our words become prayer, God will come."

Slowly, with the painful stiffness of age, he went down heavily on one knee, then on both. Knelt in the center of the aisle, facing the altar, the soles of his heavy farm boots showing from the hem of his robe. He trembled. He shut his eyes. "Let us pray."

He bent his head. "Our Father, Who art in Heaven," he said. His trembling increased. He entered null. He would never come back. In null.

He heard them kneel. "Our Father, Who art in Heaven." Relieved, their voices echoed his.

"Hallowed be Thy name," the Abbot said.

"Hallowed be Thy name."

Brian Moore, who was born and educated in Belfast, emigrated to Canada in 1948, becoming a Canadian citizen. He now resides in the United States.

Among other honours, Mr. Moore has received a Guggenheim Foundation Fellowship, an award from the National Institute of Arts and Letters in the United States, and the Governor General of Canada's Award for fiction.